THE
GEORGE
AND
DRAGON

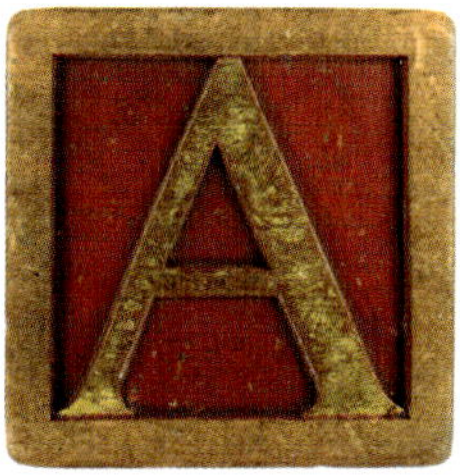

is for Ashbee

AN ARTS AND CRAFTS ALPHABET

Peyton Skipwith
& Brian Webb

Court Barn
Chipping Campden
A Museum of Craft & Design
from the Arts & Crafts movement onwards

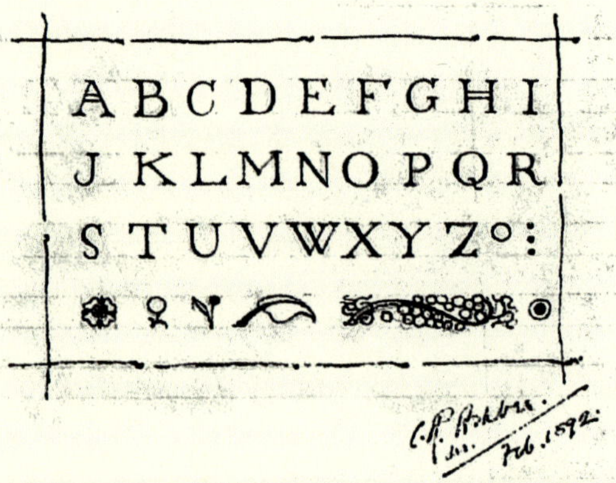
ABCDEFGHI
JKLMNOPQR
STUVWXYZ
C.R. Ashbee.
Feb. 1892

'Dreams may not stand the test of reason, but why should we not inaugurate the renaissance of make-believe by insisting upon reason standing the test of dreams?'

Holbrook Jackson, *Romance and Reality*, London 1911[1]

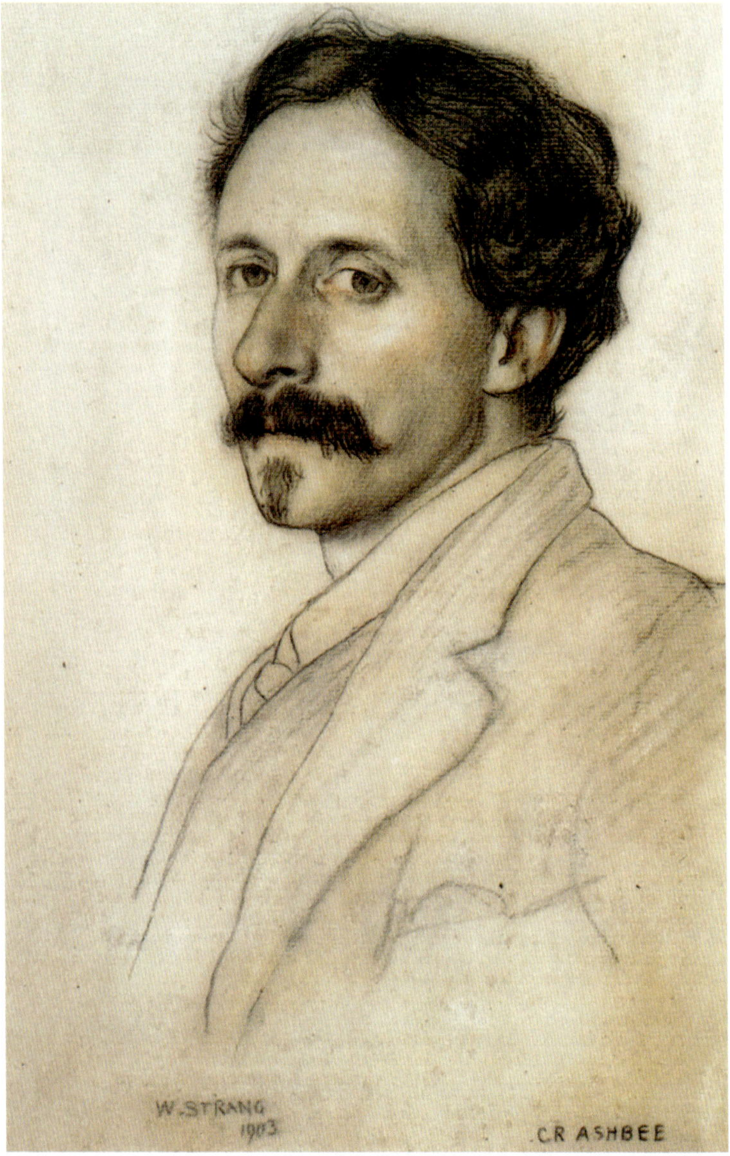
W. STRANG
1903
CR ASHBEE

FOREWORD

In September 2015 I was invited to give the annual C.R. Ashbee lecture in Chipping Campden, the erstwhile home of the Guild of Handicraft and still home to its heirs, including the Hart family of silversmiths. Chipping Campden, along with Sapperton and other corners of the Cotswolds, lies at the very core of what traditionally we regard as the heart of the English Arts & Crafts Movement, so what could I possibly talk about that the Campden audience wouldn't have heard a hundred times before? I chose, whilst being serious, to be intentionally provocative. Inspired by Ashbee's 1892 sheet of lettering I decided to create an Arts and Crafts Alphabet, embracing the comfortable and well-known as well as the outrageous and nearly unthinkable. For this purpose I rejigged and updated J.D. Sedding's peroration to the 1888 Liverpool Arts Congress: 'We should have had no Morris, no Street, no Burges, no Shaw, no Webb, no Bodley, no Rossetti, no Burne-Jones, no Crane but for Pugin.' Fast-forwarding it to read: 'We should have had no Ashbee, no Frampton, no Lutyens, no Gill, no Voysey, no Johnston, no Corbusier, no Mendelsohn, no Wright, no Gropius, but for Morris.' Brian Webb and I have compiled this book for Court Barn Museum in the same spirit, in the hope that this light-hearted approach will give pleasure, interspersed with occasional bouts of apoplexy, but above all in the hope that it will provoke thought and discussion.

Peyton Skipwith

William Strang (1859–1921) *C.R. Ashbee*, 1903

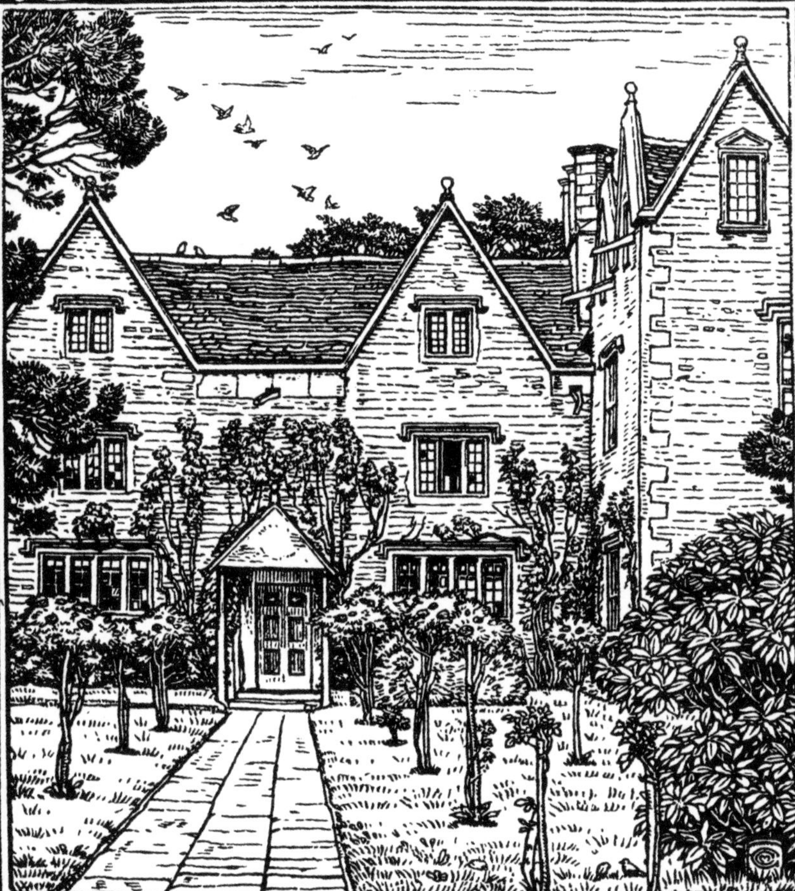

THIS IS THE PICTURE OF THE OLD
HOUSE BY THE THAMES TO WHICH
THE PEOPLE OF THIS STORY WENT
HEREAFTER FOLLOWS THE BOOK IT-
SELF WHICH IS CALLED NEWS FROM
NOWHERE OR AN EPOCH OF REST &
IS WRITTEN BY WILLIAM MORRIS

A IS FOR ASHBEE...

We all think we know what the Arts & Crafts Movement is, or was, but do we? Was it an urban or a rural movement? An English, British or international movement? An idealistic or a practical movement? Was it merely a period in past design history or is it a still vital movement? These are all valid questions, and to confuse matters further, as Kipling wrote:

There are nine and sixty ways of constructing tribal lays.
And – every – single – one – of – them – is – right.

The Arts & Crafts was definitely rural in most of its practice, but the drive from the cities provided much of the impetus; without the urban pressure resulting from the reaction against the worst exploitive effects of the Industrial Revolution – the grime and overcrowding, the use of sham materials and the sham techniques of manufacture – the Arts & Crafts Movement would have lacked much of its vitality as well as its intellectual content. Yes, it was an English movement in origin and, in architectural terms, apart from the fourteenth-fifteenth century Perpendicular – Pevsner's beloved 'Perp' – it is the only truly home-grown style. Yes, it was both an idealistic and a practical movement, and, yes, in terms of design The Arts & Crafts Movement – with capital letters – was an historic movement of the late nineteenth century, but its antecedents were rooted in earlier centuries of English life and custom. Kenneth Clark in his lecture, 'Is the Artist Ever Free?', drew a comparison

Wood-engraved frontispiece for *News From Nowhere*, by William Morrris, from Charles Gere's drawing of Kelmscott Manor, Kelmscott Press, 1892

between the history of art and nature: 'If any natural analogy is to be used (and none will be exact) it is more like a series of harvests some of which are self-sown, so that the crop gets progressively poorer; and some which are sown afresh, and the seed is individual genius.'[2] In the second half of the nineteenth century, with regard to the Arts & Crafts, Ruskin and Morris provided that individual genius sowing 'the seed afresh', to use Clark's phrase. But Arts & Crafts is more than just a style, it is an idealistic and enduring ethic, with no precise beginning, and certainly no end; its ideals, though frequently neglected, are as valid today as they were a century-and-a-half ago. If it had a precise, pin-pointable beginning it would probably be somewhere in the Middle Ages with the carvers and glaziers, much of whose work still adorns our great cathedrals, or those inspired Nottingham sculptors who created the alabaster groups, which are among the glories of mediaeval England. Alternatively it could be regarded as having its roots in the late sixteenth or early seventeenth century with the silversmiths, embroiderers and stuccoists. Mary Sloane depicted May Morris in the tapestry room at Kelmscott hung with pieces from the seventeenth century, though Morris himself derived much of his inspiration for his Merton Abbey tapestries from the great French fifteenth-century *mille-fleurs* examples in the Musée de Cluny in Paris, with which he was familiar.

And what about the present and the future? Although lacking the venerability of age are not Prue Cooper's slipware dishes as witty and lively as those of her eighteenth century Devonian predecessors? It will be a sad day if there comes a time when there is no one to sow the harvest afresh and mankind looses faith in the aspirations embodied in the Utopian philosophy which lies at the heart of the Movement. Though I must admit my heart sank on a recent visit to the newly reopened Design Museum where I witnessed a 3D printer at work programmed by Olivier Vantlerpt and Sander Wassink of Adaptive Manufacturing. The accompanying

18th century Barnstaple Slipware Jug (top): 21st century Slipware Dish by Prue Cooper (bottom) Mary Sloane, *May Morris in the Tapestry Room at Kelmscott Manor, 1912* (overleaf)

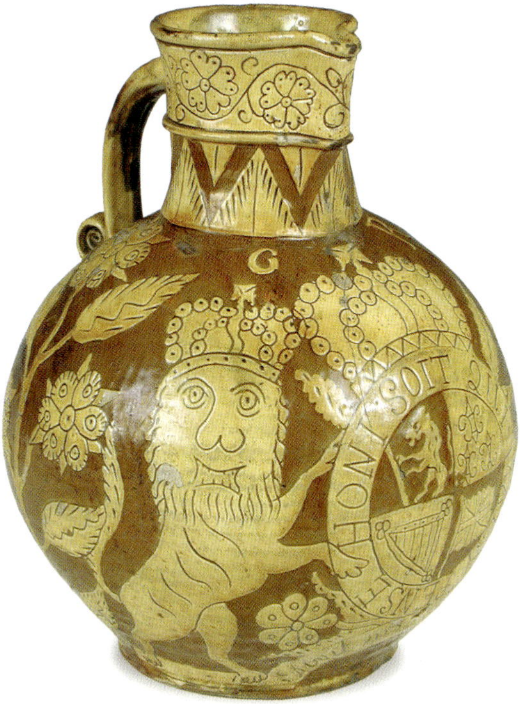

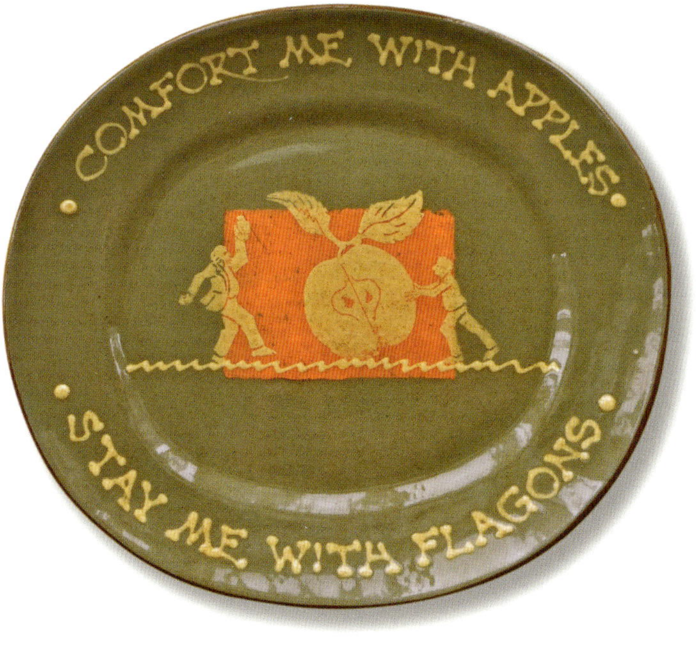
COMFORT ME WITH APPLES
STAY ME WITH FLAGONS

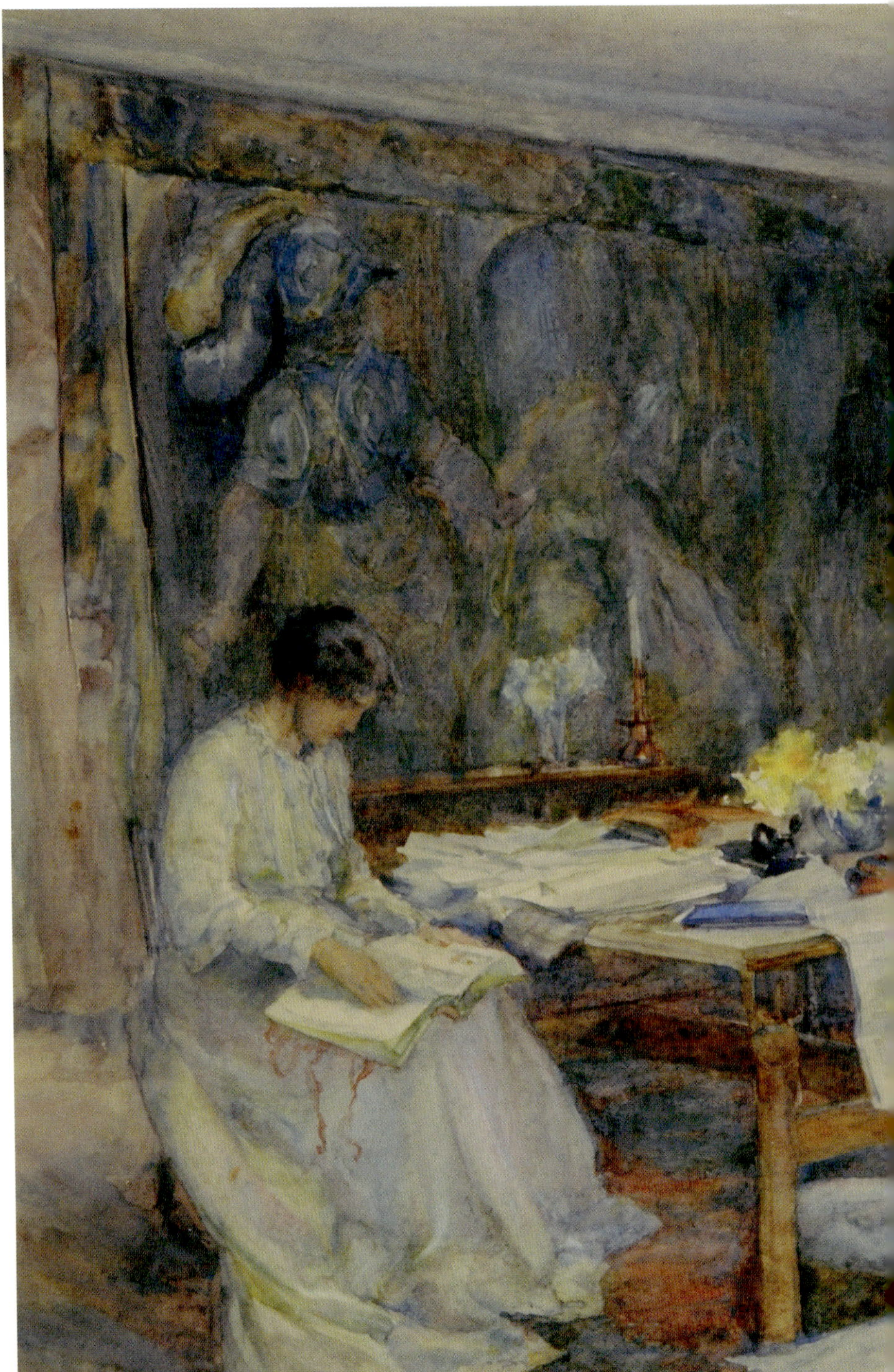

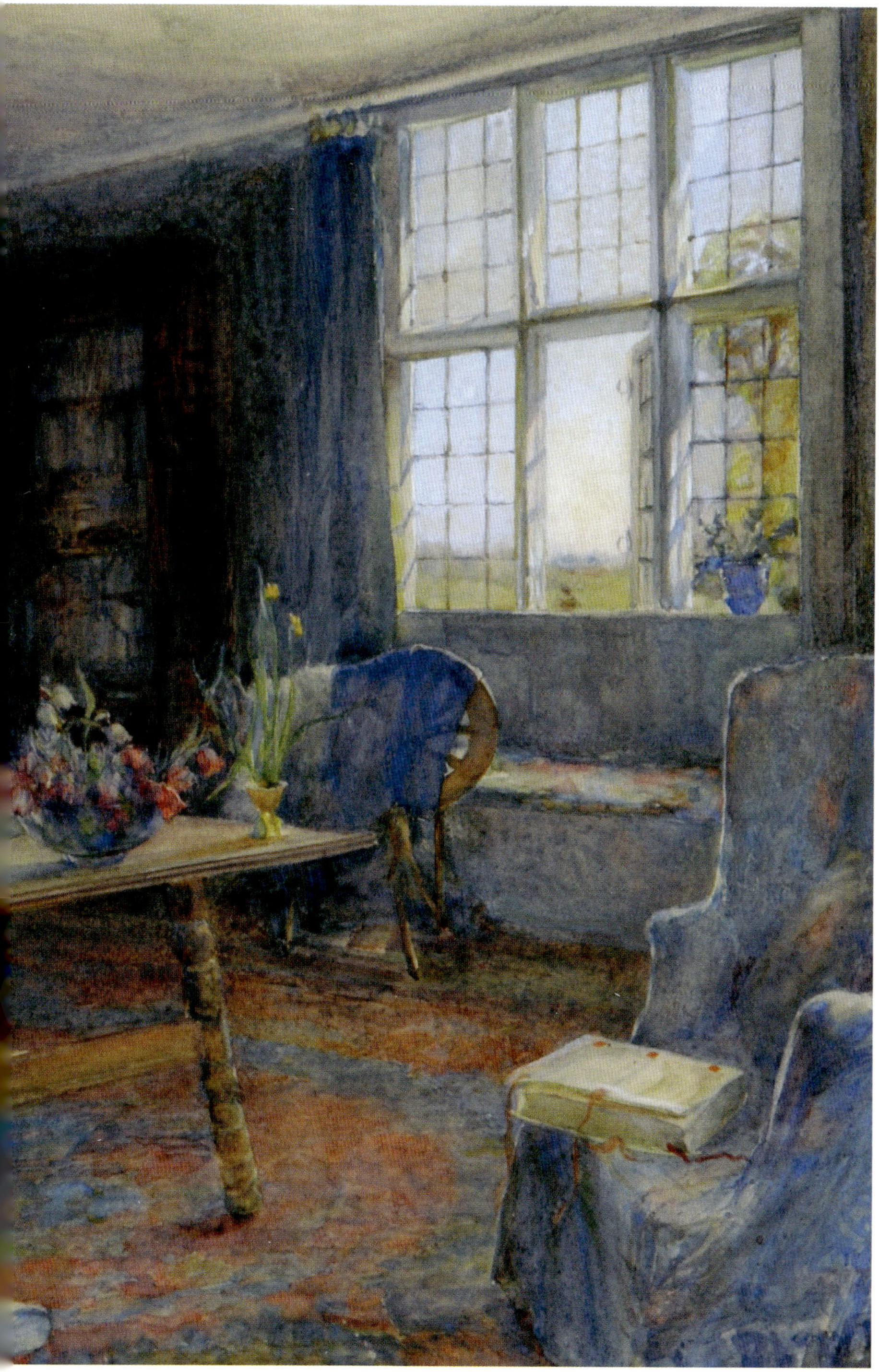

text stated that it had been 'conceived to bring the qualities of crafted objects, the sense of human input and local relevance to digital manufacturing.'

What we define today as the historic Arts and Crafts Movement covers a period roughly between 1870 and the outbreak of the First World War. Its birth and origins were thoroughly English, stretching back to a tranquil, pre-industrial age, revitalised by the example of Pugin and his followers with the addition of the powerful moral preaching of Ruskin and Morris. Their cry was quickly taken up by others, and the very Englishness of the movement was recognised and seized upon by other ethnic groups – Scots, Irish, Hungarians, Austrians, Fins – all, unlike their English counterparts, with perceived grudges against the powers by which they were ruled. The subtle use of national symbols and materials – cairngorms for jewellery, Celtic designs on metalwork, etc. all harking back to a semi-mythical golden age – became subtly subversive nationalistic statements. Just as early in the last century brooches and other items of jewellery made up of green,

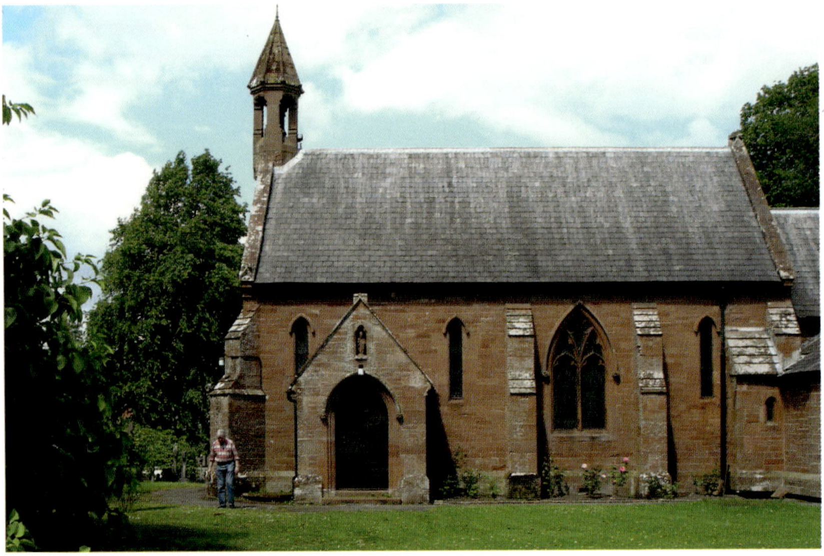

Our Lady & St Wilfred's Church, 1840–41, Warwick Bridge, Cumbria, A.W.N. Pugin (1812–1852)

white and purple stones – the colours of the Women's Social and Political Union – declared the wearer to be a supporter of the suffragettes.

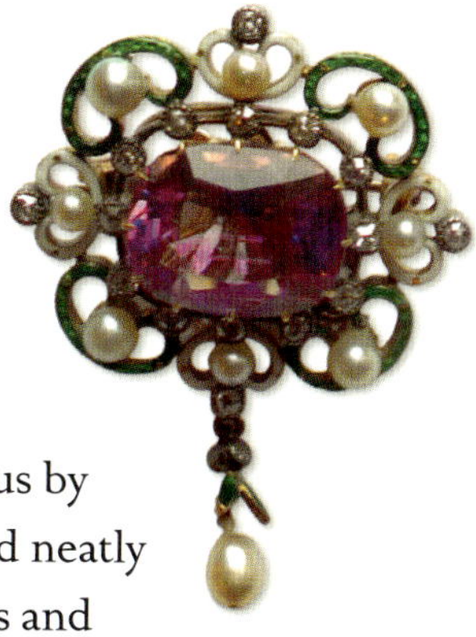

Nikolaus Pevsner in his brilliantly argued *Pioneers of Modern Design* states in the introduction that 'the phase between Morris and Gropius is an historical unit.'[3] Thus by wrapping up the Arts & Crafts Movement and neatly pigeonholing it, he pronounced its obsequies and virtually consigned it to history. An honourable and worthy history, but history none-the-less. The importance to him of Morris, Burne-Jones, Lewis F. Day, Walter Crane, Harrison Townsend, Alfred Gilbert, Voysey, Ashbee and Gimson, was that they were Pioneers. They were like a body of John the Baptists, all presaging the arrival of the Messiah or, in this case Walter Gropius. In stressing their rôle he de-coupled them from the Arts & Crafts and linked them instead to the Modern Movement. They became stepping-stones towards Modernism, a glorious era in which the brutalism of Breuer was to hold prime place. 'The engineers stand at the entrance of the new style', he declared, quoting Henri van der Velde, 'Engineers are "the architects of the present day"'. [4] In this march of technical progress he ignored the ethical core of the Arts & Crafts Movement: for him and other protagonists of the Modern Movement, functionalism was the prime motivating impulse, in direct contrast to Morris who firmly believed that it was 'not possible to dissociate art from morality, politics and religion.' [5]

Modernism would have happened regardless of the Arts and Crafts, as it was driven in large part by the availability of new materials, but despite this the influence of Ruskin, Morris and the Arts and Crafts Movement on the Deutscher Werkbund was seminal. At the end of the nineteenth century the German government attached such importance to English architecture and design that they assigned Hermann Muthesius to their embassy in

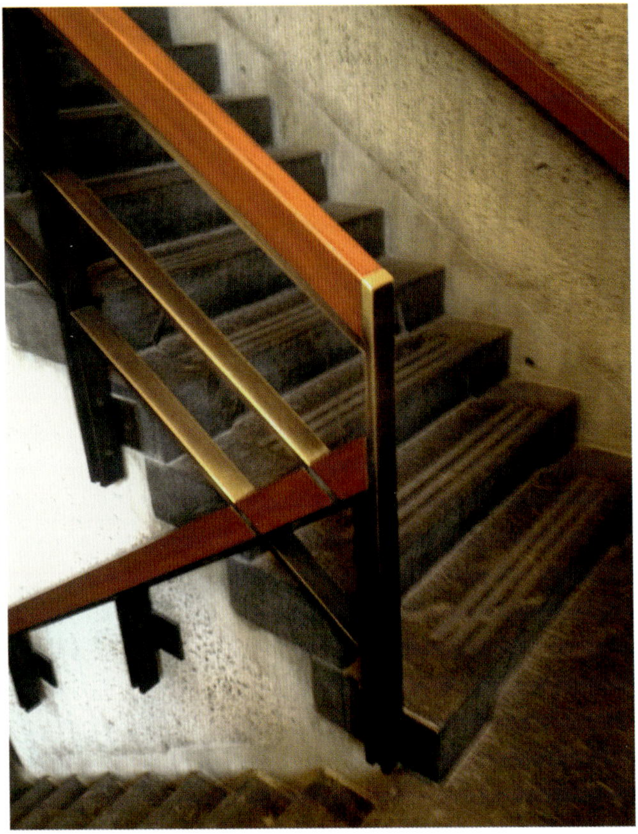

Marcel Breuer (1902–1981) Corner of staircase in the Met Breuer, New York, 1966

London to study it, and make a full report in order to raise standards at home. Being a thorough nation the Germans took his reports to heart and by the early years of the twentieth century their products, such as Van der Velde's *sang-de-boeuf* vase [p. 78], were surpassing in quality those of their British exemplars. This is partly explained by the fact that they did not share the hang-ups that obsessed many of their British counterparts, particular the belief that hand-making was intrinsically superior to machine manufacture. However not all the Arts & Crafts men did either. Christopher Dresser and W.A.S. Benson for instance were as much masters of the machine as any of their German confrères, and were just as reliant on the precision of their metal-turning machines for their lamps and teapots as

Marianne Brandt was to be for hers. Even Ashbee acknowledged that machinery was necessary for modern production, though like Morris himself he railed against its abuse, as is clear from his pronouncement that 'machinery in so far as it destroys human individuality is bad, in so far as it develops it it is good.'[6]

Nikolaus Pevsner felt that England had abrogated to Germany its leadership in 'shaping the new style just about 1900, that is, at the very moment when the work of all the pioneers began to converge into one universal movement.'[7] Certainly by the early years of the twentieth century the phenomenon of internationalism was beginning to set in, and those members of the Art Workers' Guild and others who defied the growing mood of belligerency to visit the 1914 Cologne Exhibition came home deeply impressed by the work produced by members of the Deutscher Werkbund. This resulted in an extraordinary event. In March 1915, despite the war, the British Government, through the Board of Trade, sponsored an exhibition at Goldsmiths' Hall in the heart of the City of well-designed German manufactures, resulting within a matter of months in the setting up of the Design and Industries Association (DIA) under the chairmanship of Lord Aberconway. This breakdown not only of national boundaries, but also of national character, and characteristics, was seemingly inexorable, enabling Herbert Read to write in his introduction to *Unit One* a couple of decades later, that 'In architecture, and in sculpture, as well as in painting, a new awareness of the real purpose or function of the arts has been slowly evolved during the last fifty years, and this consciousness is international in its extent. Whatever happens in England will be part of what is happening in Europe and America generally.'[8]

C.F.A. Voysey, another giant of the Arts and Crafts was happy to have his fire surrounds, hinges, door-handles, etc. manufactured by such firms as Comyn, Ching, Thomas Elsley, and the Falkirk Iron Company so that they could be ordered in the desired quantities when required, to give those added personal touches to the houses he designed for his clients. He was also quite cavalier in selling his designs for wallpapers, textiles and carpets to various manufacturers, thus abrogating his right of control over their production. In contrast of course to this commercialism, or semi-industrialisation, of the Arts and Crafts there were other craftsmen who revelled in handwork and the tactility of their craft. Sidney Barnsley delighted in the physical activity of sawing tree trunks into planks, while his son, Edward, often quoted D.H. Lawrence's lines:

'Things men have made with wakened hands,
and put soft life into
Are awake through years with transferred touch,
and go on glowing
For long years.'

But Edward was as physical as his father, even to the extent of digging a swimming pool in the garden of his workshop-cum-cottage at Froxfield, and in old age his widow Tania's eyes would light up as she recalled her first sight of her future husband, stripped to the waist, on the scaffold of the Gimson-designed Memorial Library at Bedales School. Bedales, like Abbotsholme, had been founded on Arts and Crafts principles, and it was at the latter that the young Harold Curwen was first inculcated with Morris's ideals, which later made him into one of the most creative printers of his generation. Ironically this new-found veneration for the 'life beautiful' which these schools preached helped at the same time, and to some degree, to bring those principles into disrepute. Edward Thomas's wife, Helen, who taught for a while at Bedales, recalled her fellow teachers thus: 'None of them were rich, but none were poor... they all –

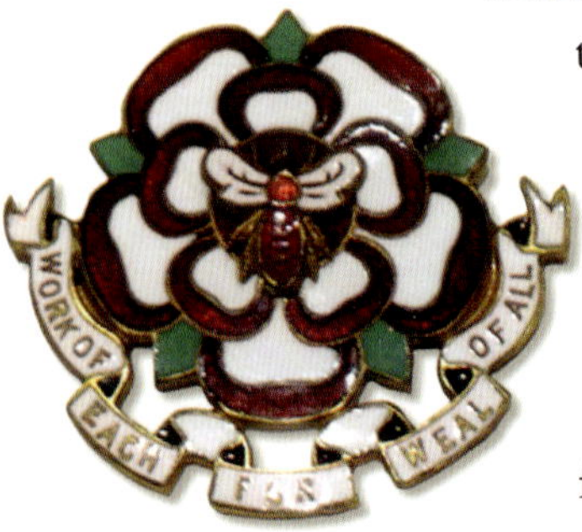

The Bedales' Bee enamel cap badge (above), Harold Curwen's 'Get the Spirit of Joy', 1920, decorated by Claud Lovat Fraser (opposite)

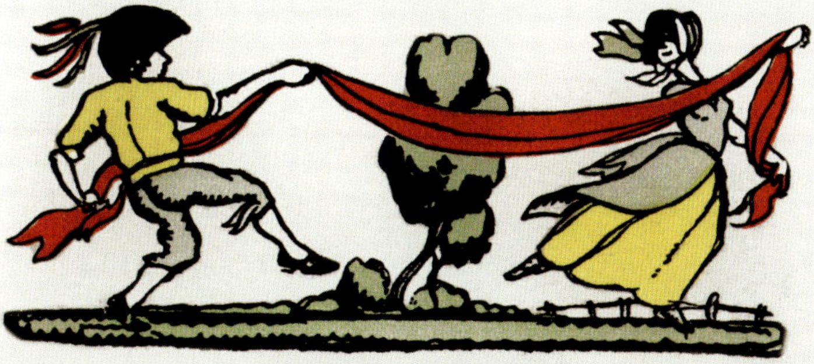

GET THE

SPIRIT OF JOY

INTO YOUR PRINTED THINGS

THE WORLD'S dead tired of drab dullness in Business Life.

GIVE your customers credit for a sense of Humour and some Understanding.

TAKE your courage in both hands and have your printing done

CHEERILY!

I arrange & make
COURAGEOUS PRINTING
At the Curwen Press
Plaistow, London, E.13
Harold Curwen

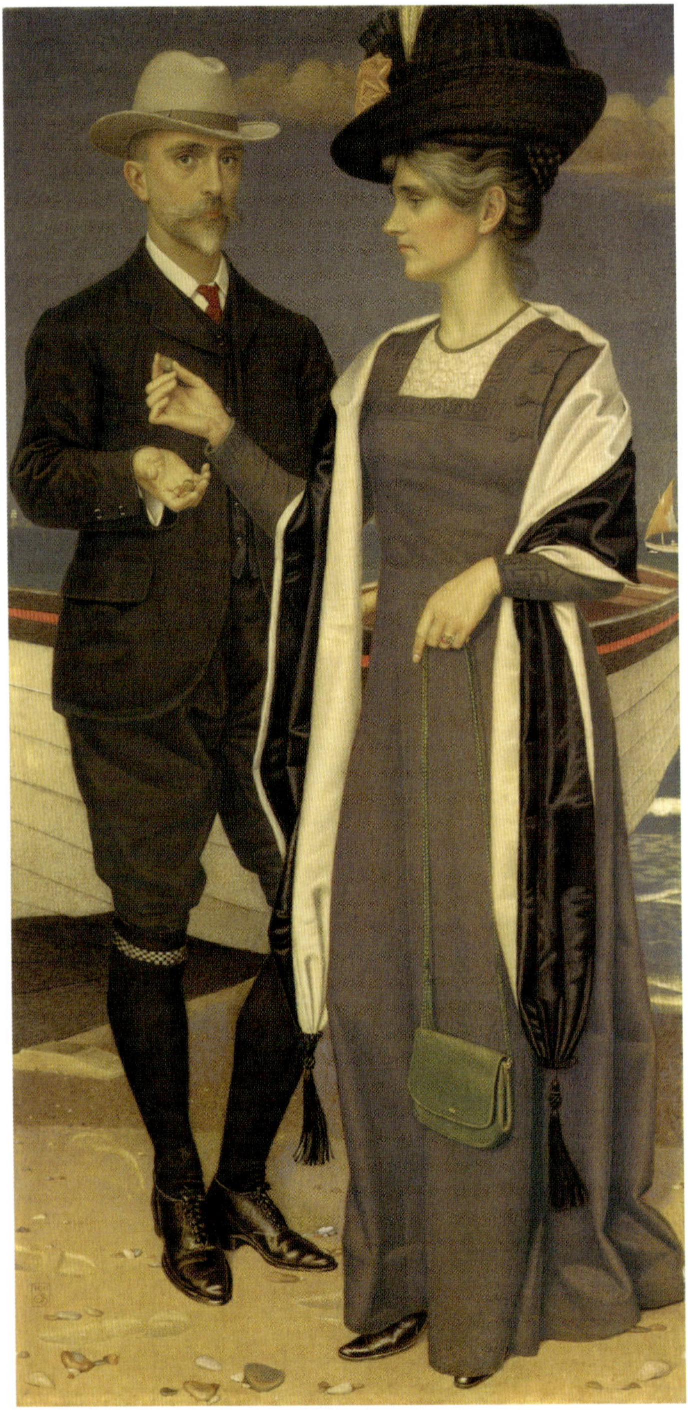

so it seemed to me – had led and would always lead the same quiet comfortable lives, rational, well balanced. Their politics inclined to Socialism and they were on more than usual friendly terms with the villagers... they were moderate in all things; they read the best books and the *Manchester Guardian,* and loved the best music, and had replicas of the best pictures on their walls. Their homes were in faultless taste outside and in. Their simple oak furniture was made by skilled craftsmen, and their curtains were hand-woven. Their meals were lavish and good, inclining to brown bread and vegetarianism and, of course, non-alcoholic.'[9] A speedy road to constipation, both mental and corporal.

The thought of such admirable but desiccated worthiness would probably have been approved, among others, by the tempera painter Joseph Southall and his wife Bessie and their fellow Birmingham Quakers, but it would have appalled the full-blooded Morris, a trencherman who exchanged gifts of claret with Frederick Engels. Moderation was not in his nature, he would have been more at home under the roof of Walter Scott's character Luckie Dods at the Cleikum in Aulton of St Ronan's than round the table of those worthy teachers. Much of his mediaevalism was inspired by Scott's tales of chivalry, and he had read all the Waverley novels – including *St Ronan's Well* – by the time he was eight. He rejoiced in Scott's devotion to the antique Gaelic dialect as well as to Anglo-Saxon epithets, just as he did in the direct language of the Icelandic Sagas. He revelled in descriptions of scenes of blood, guts, rapine and pillage, as much as in their redemption by acts of valour and chivalry. His own language could be just as earthy, as witnessed here in E. Belfort Bax's account, as recalled by his son, of Burne-Jones taking W.B Yeats, the budding young Irish poet, to supper at Kelmscott House after a meeting of the Hammersmith Socialist Society. [p. 85] Morris could swear like a bargee and was as irascible as a porcupine, and 'his capacity

Joseph Southall (1861–1944) *The Agate,* 1911

in the art of the expletive was as vigorous as his vocabulary was original and varied.' as Holbrook Jackson tells us.[10] A cartoon in *Fun* following the debacle of Bloody Sunday – 13th November 1887 – when the Home Secretary sent mounted and armed troops to break up a workers' demonstration in Trafalgar Square, shows Morris holding a banner inscribed 'The Earthly Paradox', while a policeman polishes his shoes. The paradox of Morris is perhaps most vividly illustrated by his French edition of Marx's *Das Kapital* which he had sumptuously bound by Cobden-Sanderson. [p. 57]

The influence of history and romance on Morris and his circle – Malory's *Morte d'Arthur*, Walter Scott's Waverley Novels, Ruskin's devotion to thirteenth-century gothic, and the ubiquitous example of Pugin in Britain and Violet-le-Duc across the Channel – was overpowering. Philip Webb's Red House at Bexleyheath for Morris, with its quasi-mediaeval furnishings and chairs 'fit for a Barbarossa', makes one seriously question when the 'arts and crafts' began. Was it in the Middle Ages, or in the reign of Queen Elizabeth I, or, as has been suggested with Morris in the thirteenth century? Or could it just have been a late flowering of age-old, but ongoing, traditions, a continuation of craft-skills that had never died out? Was it a growth that had for a time been obscured and overlaid by the Industrial Revolution and changing fashions? Or was it in Clark's words a crop that had gradually got 'progressively poorer', but never quite extinguished?

In 1921 John Drinkwater in *Cotswold Characters*, eulogised the Gloucestershire countryside high above the great Stroud Valley: 'the neighbourhood of the famous wool-staplers of the sixteenth century, when the Cotswold flocks brought those merchants to a prosperity which they spent partly making themselves noble dwelling-places out of the lovely Cotswold stone. The country then bred a great race of masons, and the stock has never died out.' He went on to describe his own home: ' a small cottage on a byway that is passed by a stranger hardly once a week. It is four rooms big. Eighty years ago [1860] two of them were built by a local craftsman

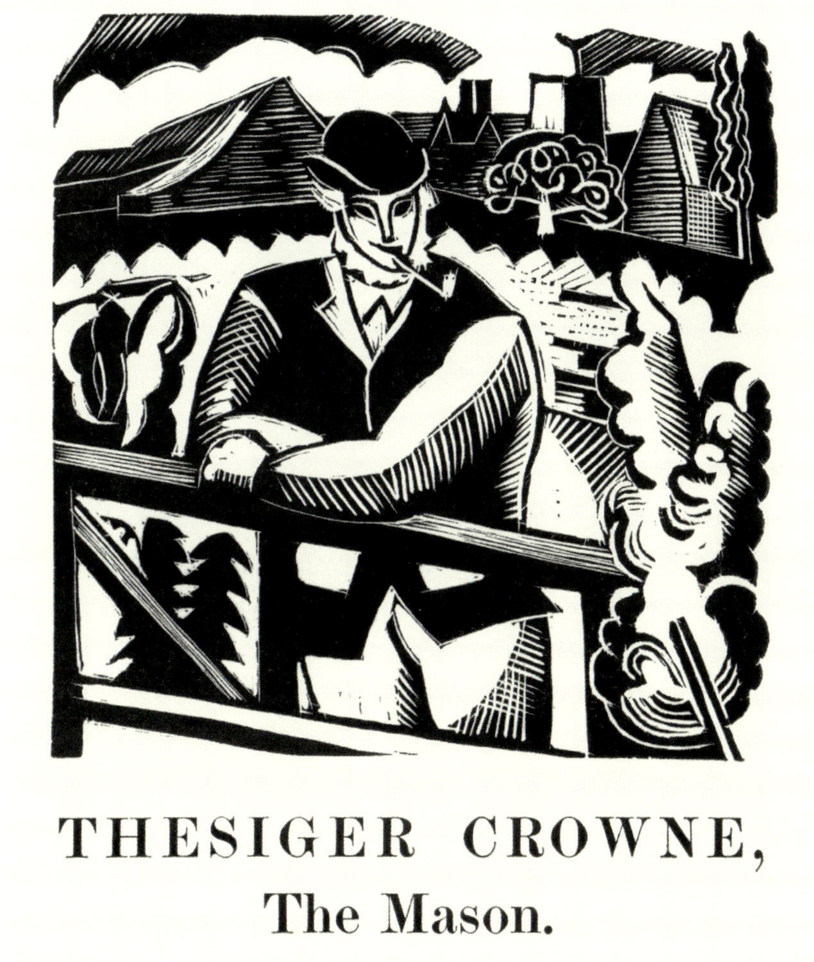

Wood engraving by Paul Nash (1889–1946) for *Cotswold Characters* by John Drinkwater, 1921

who knew neither better nor worse than his ancestors nearly three hundred years back. And then ten years ago my landlord added the other two, and he, again, worked with the same unquestioning and perfect mastery. So it is that the whole countryside is covered with an architecture which has never lost its vitality. it is not a question of copying with skill a fine tradition gone by. Here we have, rather, the real life which consists of a personal contribution to a tradition that has never died out.'[11] Paul Nash, who illustrated the work, depicted one of Drinkwater's characters, the seventy-seven-year-old mason Thesiger Crowne, who had carried on these old traditions and had worked as far away as Sussex and Norfolk.

It was natural that craft traditions had been carried on undisturbed in places remote from the great cities. 'Happily, instinctive qualities are not easily exterminated, and may lie dormant until the genial season returns which is to quicken them to life. This hope is indeed strongly supported by cultured craftsmen friends, like the late Mr Ernest Gimson for instance, who have tapped professionally the strictly rural population for the purposes of artistic handicraft work, and have found native genius in plenty ready to respond to a fostering touch.'[12] The Industrial Revolution and the coming of the railways had speeded up the migration from country to town, but city life left men 'no time to stand and stare', or to cultivate their own garden plots and keep a chicken or two. It was only in the remoter regions – remote from the railways particularly – that the pace of life continued in its old, leisurely manner, governed by the seasons, with craft traditions handed down from generation to generation. Many of those who had migrated to the cities looked patronisingly on their country cousins who retained their quaint old ways, treating them with affectionate toleration; Flora Thompson gives such an insight into this in *Lark Rise to Candleford.*

It was not until the middle of the nineteenth century that a reaction began to set in and some of the younger scions of newly wealthy city manufacturers, industrialists and merchants – Morris, Gimson, the Barnsleys, Ashbee, Carpenter – woke up to the danger of what they were losing. But a prerequisite to such a 'waking up' was first having the luxury to sleep and dream. As Holbrook Jackson so wisely wrote: 'Hours of voluntary idleness are indeed hours of praise. For in such hours we are in communion with the real world; in them we have done with the time that passeth away, and become one with the time which is eternal. The priests of old knew

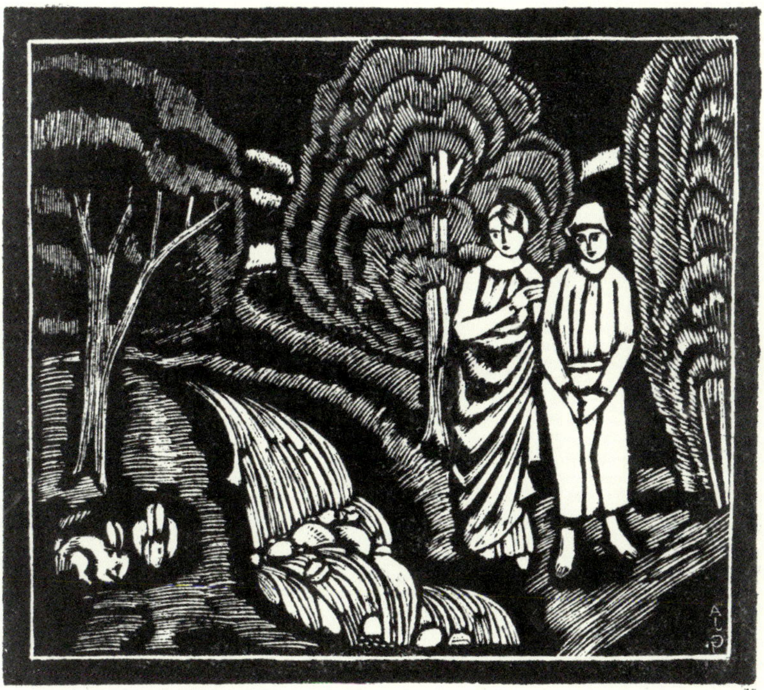

Arthur Gaskin (1862–1928) Engraved headpiece *To Idleness* by Christoper Whitfield

this when they instructed their acolytes in the art of meditation. Walt Whitman knew it when he loafed on "fish-shaped Paumanok" observing a spear of summer grass; Thoreau knew it in his hut by Walden Pond; William Blake knew it when he saw the angels on Peckham Rye.'[13] Christopher Whitfield, a young Birmingham industrialist who escaped to Chipping Campden, knew it when he penned his poem *To Idleness* which was embellished with a wood engraving by Arthur Gaskin and became the first production of the Shakespeare Head Press.

Drinkwater's Thesiger Crowne may have taken his masonry skills across the country, but other craftsmen – Philip Clissett and the elder Bucknell among them – remained in their respective corners, where their forebears had lived for generations. Clissett was a traditional Worcestershire chair bodger, who, as D.S McColl

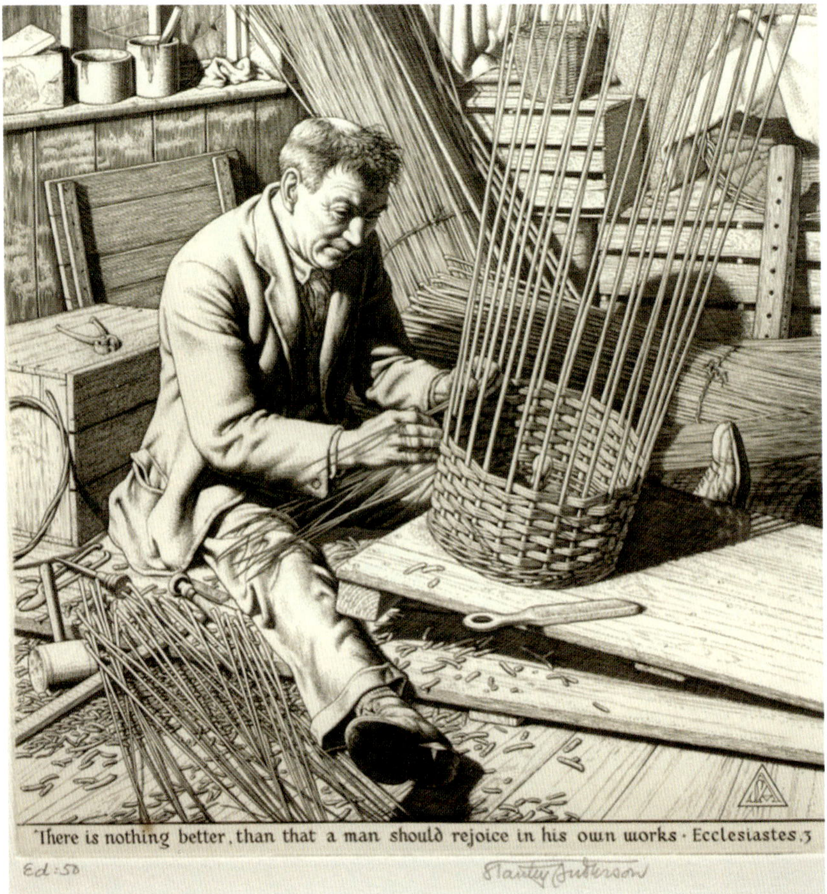

Stanley Anderson (1884–1966) *The Basket-Maker*

described, 'made rush-bottomed chairs with no other apparatus than his cottage oven for bending the wood.'[14] Bucknell was the blacksmith in the Gloucestershire village of Waterlane whose son, Alfred, Gimson set up with his own smithy in the wheelwright's yard at Sapperton. Many of these crafts, chair-, hurdle-, and basket-making among them, were later recorded in a remarkable series of engravings by Stanley Anderson, himself the son of an heraldic engraver, who became a noted Royal Academician. Some crafts withered naturally as demand for their product decreased but others such as the making of chairs, baskets, and decorative ironwork took on a new lease. The Scots architect, James McLaren, met Clissett in the mid-1880s and suggested a modification to the design of his traditional rush-seated, spindle-backed chair, which was later bought in quantity by the Art Workers' Guild for use in their hall, then in Barnard's Inn off the Strand. They cost 10/6 each (55 pence in today's currency); they were also later retailed at a somewhat higher price through Heal's in Tottenham Court Road. Heal's is an interesting example of an old established family firm of bed manufacturers which, under the enlightened guidance of a younger family member – Ambrose – was to transform itself into a high end producer and purveyor of arts and crafts style furniture, under the supervision of C.V Adams, who had been Ashbee's foreman cabinet maker. When they received large batch orders such as that which resulted from the Letchworth Cheap Cottages Exhibition of 1905, they were contracted out to other manufacturers based in Camden Town. Ambrose Heal's cousin, Cecil Brewer, designed the firm's store as well as the Mary Ward Settlement in nearby Tavistock Place, the latter in conjunction with his partner Dunbar Smith. Both Heal and Brewer were founder members of the Design and Industries Association.

Thomas Okey, who was Master of the Art Worker's Guild in 1914 when it moved into its new premises in Queen Square, Bloomsbury, was, like his father, a practising basket-maker, though in a remarkable upwardly mobile career he became the first professor of Italian at Oxford. A true autodidact, who achieved the transition from London's East End to the heights of academe in the 'city of dreaming spires.' Such duality between craft and profession among art workers was wittily described by William Allingham in a letter to Rossetti: 'Morris means to become an architect, and to that end has set about becoming a painter, at which he is making progress.'[15] Okey was proud of his basket-making and when George Clausen, a fellow-guildsman, painted his portrait he included, like a heraldic device, a half-woven basket in the top right-hand corner, in the manner of his Elizabethan and Jacobean predecessors. The instance of the professor-cum-basketmaker – or rather in Okey's case the basket-maker-cum-professor – points up the one insuperable flaw in the sustainability of the Arts & Crafts Movement; craft work was by its very nature more expensive than machine work. Thus the crafts gradually became the prerogative of the middle classes and time-honoured traditions became self-conscious and to a degree elitist. Not to the extent of Marie Antoinette playing dairy maid, but certainly to the degree of the self-satisfaction of those members of the Bedales' staff described by Helen Thomas. Oswald Powell – a younger brother of Alfred Powell, whose painted Wedgwood china, together with that of his wife Louise, was a feature of so many Arts and Crafts homes – was Second Master at Bedales, while another brother, Malcolm, taught woodworking there as, later, did Edward Barnsley's son Jon.

If Ruskin and Morris were the prophets of the Arts and Crafts Movement – along with Walter Crane and C.R. Ashbee – William Blake and Richard Jefferies, in company with Walt Whitman were its poets and psalmists. C.F.G. Masterman, in his *Condition of England*, remarks that ' in such writings as those of William Morris and Richard Jefferies, there would appear to be a kind of foretaste of a spirit which in its acceptance and its rejoicing, may be found to build up behind the deserts of life-weariness a triumphant affirmation of the greatness of Present Things.' Quoting liberally from Jefferies he commented on 'the pageant of the moment which

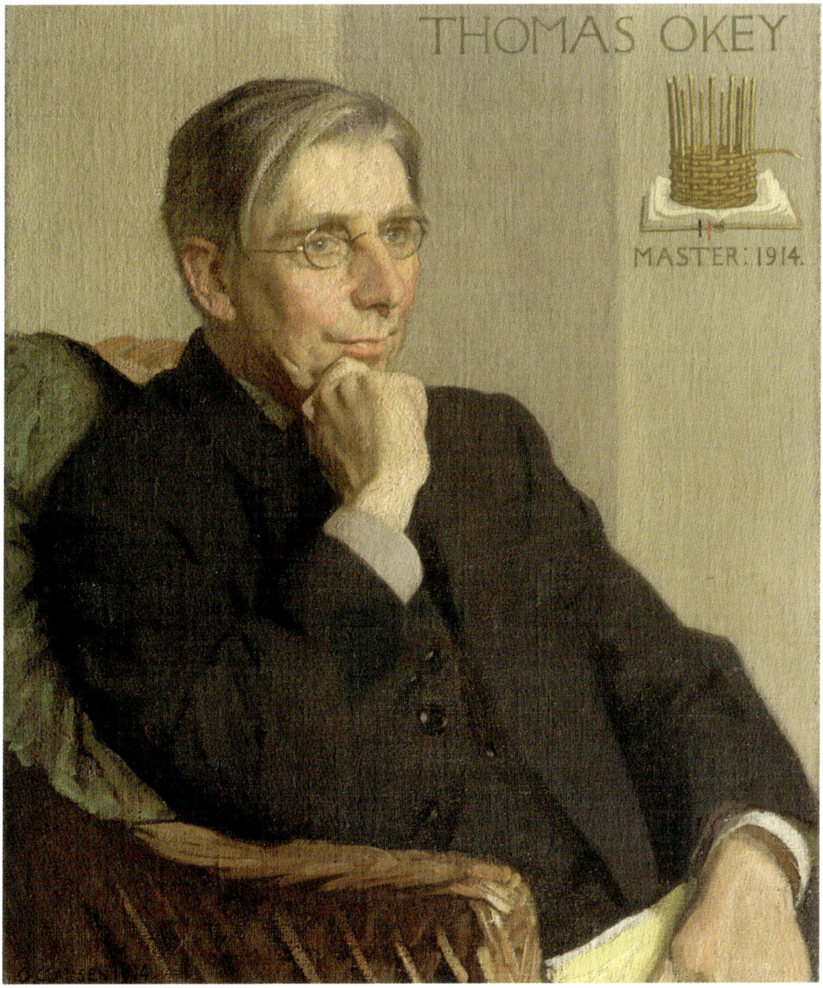

Sir George Clausen (1852–1944), *Thomas Okey*, 1914

passes and yet abides, ever old and ever young. It delights in "the old road and the same flowers." It accepts the wind's whispering that "there never was a yesterday, and never will be a tomorrow." It finds "always hope in the hills." "All the grasses of the meadow were my pets," wrote Jefferies of his childhood days. "I loved them all." Of poppies, "there is genius in them," he proclaims, "the genius of colour, and they are saved." With Thoreau he will abandon all for which most men labour to hear one cricket sing.' For Masterman Jefferies was not just a country man he was the 'worshipper of the sun, falling in the afternoon in Trafalgar Square, on the crowded Brighton promenade, in the woods of high June, or under a cold November day… For sunshine is life – riotous, confident, unashamed; life congruous to and illuminating all the physical beauty of the human body, of the world of outdoors; the life which made him almost intoxicated with the marbles in the British Museum, which drew him, resisting, to the unknown city multitudes; which left him in childhood on the downs, "utterly alone with the sun and the earth," lost in an ecstasy, an inflatus at "the inexpressible beauty of it all."'[16]

It was a shared passion for Whitman which drew together the architect Charles Holden and sculptor Jacob Epstein. Together they created one of the finest late Arts and Crafts buildings, the London headquarters of the British Medical Association in Agar Street, off the Strand – now Zimbabwe House. Epstein's monumental frieze of naked figures so roused the ire of the Philistines that they were later wilfully mutilated and stand today like those on the time worn West front of the Cathedral at Autun by Gislebertus – 'Gisel the Chisel' as he has been affectionately known to generations of stone carvers. Direct carving, especially on buildings, was an important and highly visible aspect of the Arts and Crafts Movement. J.D. Sedding, like his master, G.E. Street, would bring animals and plants into the workshop to inspire the workmen, and Eric Gill, when commissioned to make carvings of Ariel for Broadcasting House in 1931, wrote to the actor, Leslie

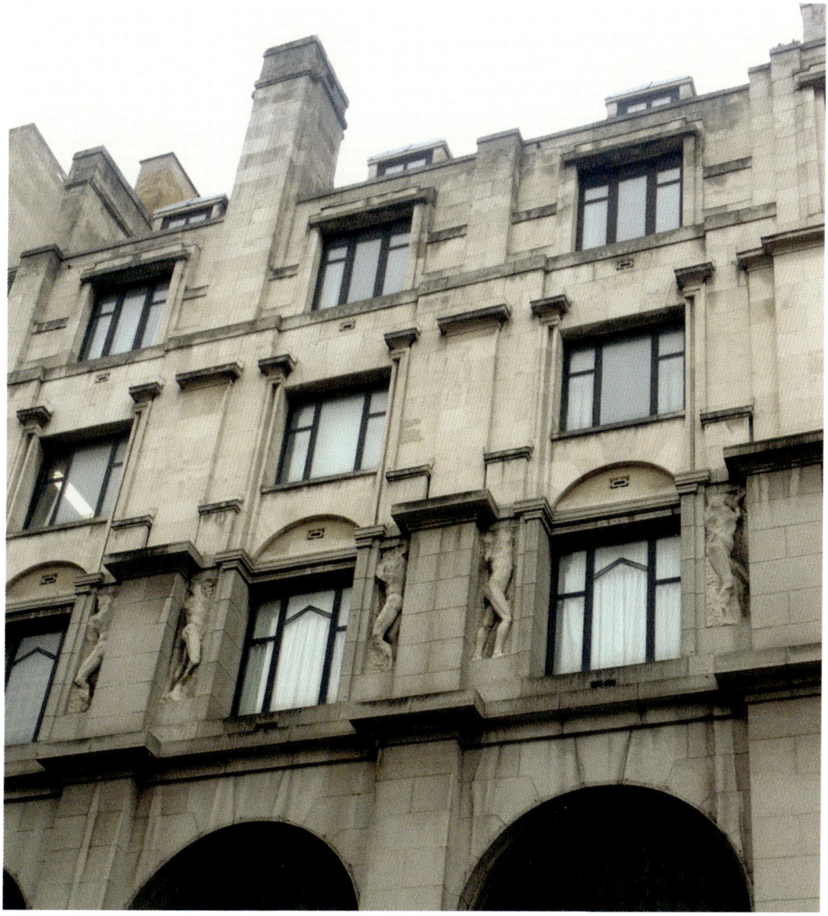

Charles Holden (1875–1960), Zimbabwe House, Agar Street, Strand, 1906–8

French, who was currently playing the part at the Old Vic, to ask whether he would allow him to 'make some studies from your beautiful figure as a help to me in making the sculpture.'[17] Many artisan carvers and modellers trained at Lambeth School of Art and the South Kensington Schools, some became well known such as the two Georges – Tinworth and Frampton – others remain largely unknown like the carver of the Green Man corbel [p. 77] though their works adorn countless buildings throughout Britain, the Commonwealth and the USA. A prime example of this sub-text of anonymous craftsmanship is the practice of Joseph Armitage who

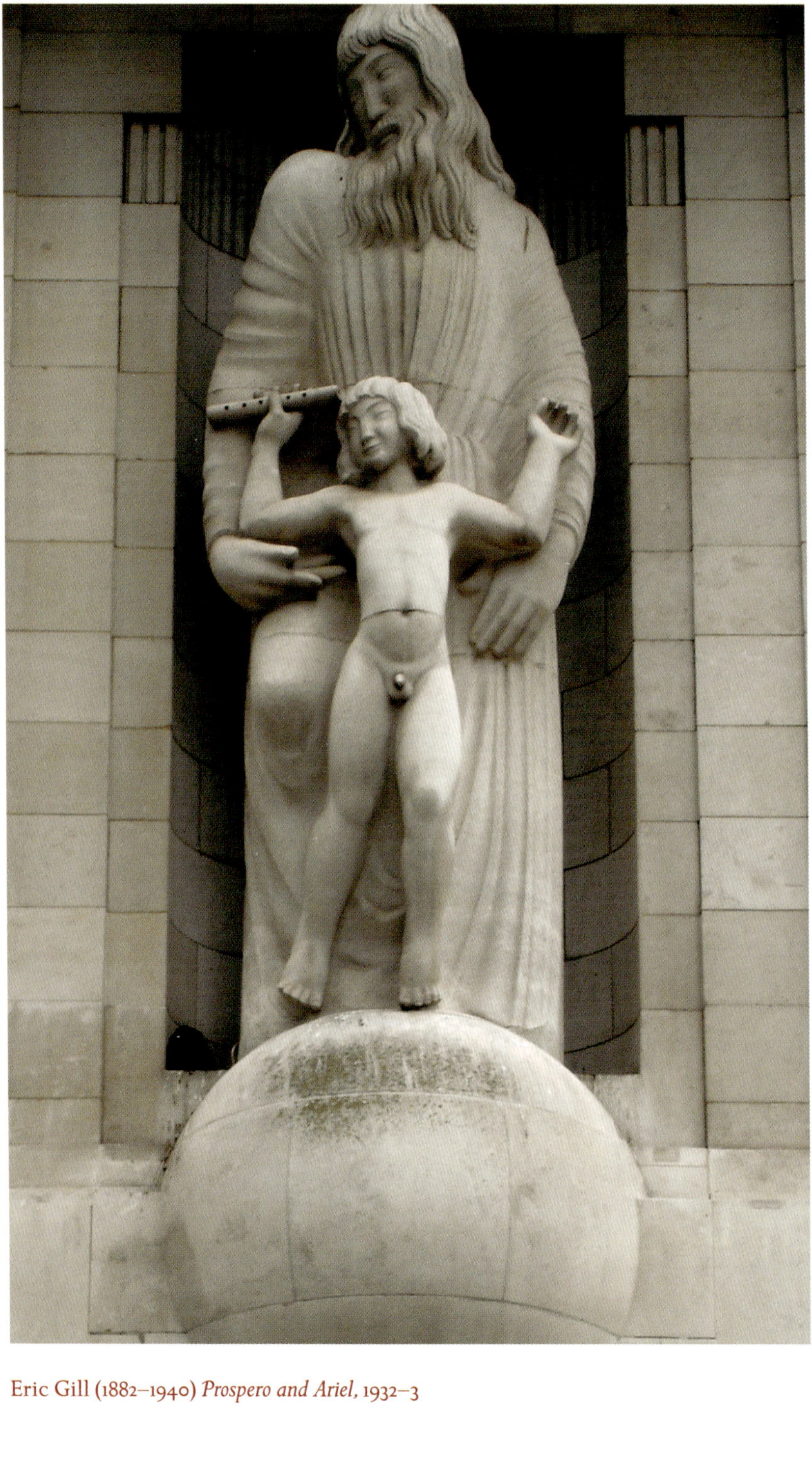

Eric Gill (1882–1940) *Prospero and Ariel*, 1932–3

was sent to New Delhi by Herbert Baker to advise on decorative carving for the new government buildings there and later, while masterminding the work at the Bank of England, was employing a hundred craftsmen – stone-carvers, woodcarvers, letter-cutters and gilders. It is such artisans as these and their predecessors – largely unrecorded and often peripatetic – who for the past thousand years and more have formed the very bedrock of the arts and crafts . It was such men – and they were almost uniquely men – who '*with wakened hands*' and '*transferred touch*', brought life to buildings ranging from the massivity of Durham Cathedral to Bodley's modest gem of All Saints, Selsley. As Ruskin wrote: 'A wall has no business to be dead. It ought to have members in its make, and purposes in its existence, like an organised creature, and to answer its ends in a living and energetic way.' [18]

It is that human quality which is at the heart of the Arts and Crafts Movement, and which was eschewed by the mainly left-wing architects of the mid-twentieth-century. A condition foreseen by Tolstoy in an essay of despair which appeared in the *Fortnightly Review* in 1909. 'The people of our Christian world live like animals, guided in their lives merely by personal interests and by their struggle with one another: differing from animals only in that the animals, from time immemorial, have kept the same stomachs, claws, and fangs, while people move with ever increasing rapidity from roads to railroads, from horses to steam, from spoken sermons and letters to printing, to telegraphs and telephones, and from sailing boats to ocean steamers, from swords to gunpowder, cannons, quick-firing guns, bombs and war aeroplanes. And life, with telegraphs, telephones, electricity, bombs, and aeroplanes, and with hatred of all for all: directed, not by some uniting spiritual principle, but, on the contrary, by animal instincts which divide, and which employ mental powers for their own satisfaction, becomes even more and more insane and wretched.' [19] Something of his vision was realised by Doris Zinkeisen in her 1944 mural panel, *The Relations of Management and Labour*, which provides the final illustration for the Alphabet.

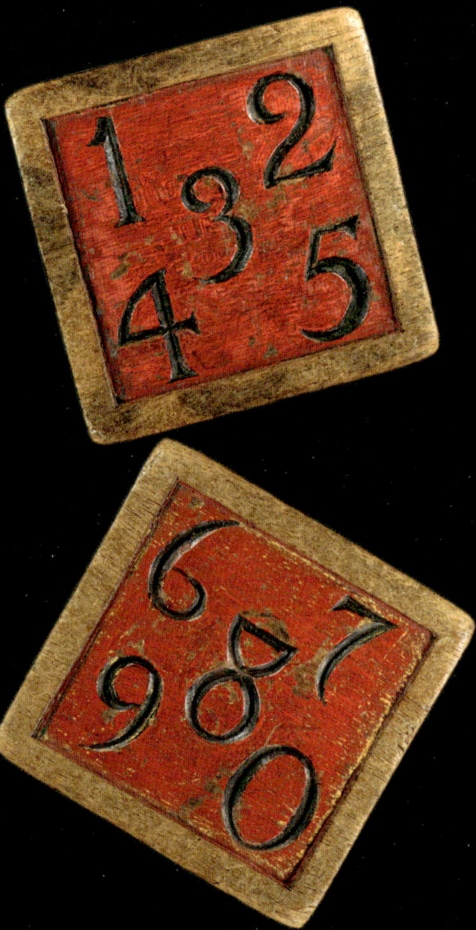
1 2
3
4 5
6
9 8 7
0

NOTES

The Alphabet blocks used throughout this book were designed by Alec Miller and carved by his brother Fred for the Ashbees' first child, Mary, in 1911 and were shown at the Arts and Crafts Exhibition Society the following year. They are on long-term loan to Court Barn.

1. Holbrook Jackson, *Romance and Reality*, London 1911, p.54
2. Quoted James Stourton, *Kenneth Clark*, William Collins, 2016, p.266
3. Pevsner, *Pioneers of Modern Design*, 1949, p.39
4. Ibid, pp. 29–30
5. *The Collected Works of William Morris*, London, 1915, xxiii, p. 147
6. Fiona MacCarthy, *The Simple Life: C.R Ashbee in the Cotswolds*, London 1981, p. 61
7. Pevsner, Op. Cit, p.175
8. Herbert Read, *Introduction, Unit One*, London 1934, p.13
9. Jean Moorcroft Wilson, *Edward Thomas: From Adlestrop to Arras*, London 2015, p. 154
10. Holbrook Jackson, *William Morris*, London 1926, p. 50
11. John Drinkwater, *Cotswold Characters*, New Haven, 1921, p. 7–8
12. Algernon Gissing, *The Footpath Way in Gloucestershire*, Dent, 1924, p.162
13. Holbrook Jackson, *Romance and Reality*, London 1911, p. 15
14. *The Architectural Review*, Vol XIII, (1903), p. 188
15. Quoted Jackson, op. cit. pp. 26–7
16. C.F.G. Masterman, *Condition of England*, Methuen, 1909, pp. 247–51
17. Ben Read & Peyton Skipwith, *Sculpture in Britain Between the Wars*, The Fine Art Society, 1986
18. Ruskin (ed. J.G. Links) *The Stones of Venice*, New York, 1960, p.45
19. Tolstoy, *Fortnightly Review*, February 1909, quoted C.F.G. Masterman, *The Condition of England*, Methuen, 1909, pp. 212–3.

ALEC MILLER (1879–1961) AND THE GUILD OF HANDICRAFT

'Only twenty-three years old, he had ten years of carving in a Glasgow workshop behind him, and had read and admired that literary production of Ashbee's London years, *A Few Chapters in Workshop Re-Construction and Citizenship*. He came to Campden unprepared for the glorious aptness of the Guild's new home, unable to read "the history embodied in those stone-built houses, so rich, so substantial, and of such beautiful stone. I simply walked on and on, in an ecstacy of pleasure, with no thought but just wonder." Alec Miller was modest and reserved, and his special qualities only revealed themselves to Ashbee slowly, his delicate skill, his creative power, above all his reading and thinking and his love for beauty. Here at last was Ashbee's ideal craftsman, the fine flower of the practical culture of the workshop, the humanistic grafted, as he had never so convincingly seen it, on to the industrial. Soaked in nineteenth-century Romantic writers, self taught with a steady, speculative cast of mind, all daylight and no dogma, Alec Miller could argue with Ashbee about Meredith and Plato, and understand the larger ideas behind the Guild. Ashbee was charmed, and at times chastened, by his tough and unpretentious clarity.'

(Alan Crawford, *C.R. Ashbee: Architect, Designer & Romantic Socialist*, Yale University Press, 1985, pp 112–3)

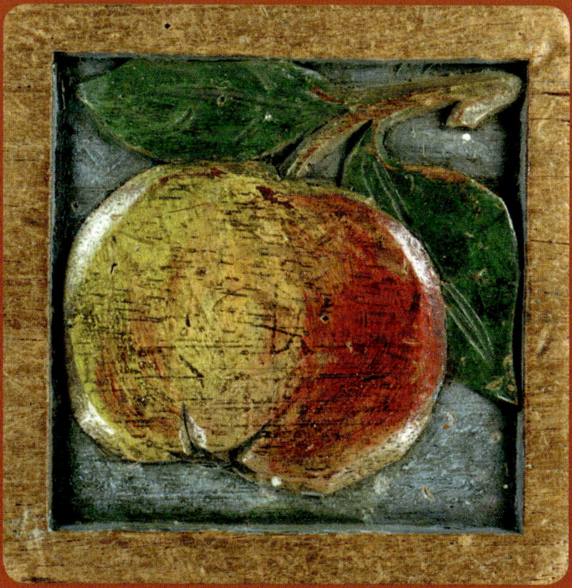

THE ALPHABET

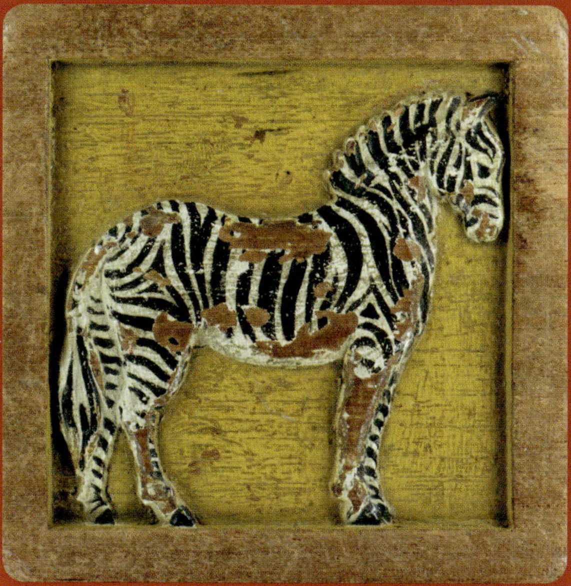

A *is for...* Aalto, Aitchison, Albert, Anderson, An Túr Gloine, Anning Bell, Anti-scrape, Armfield, Art Workers' Guild, Artificers' Guild, Ashbee, Ashendene Press & Ault.

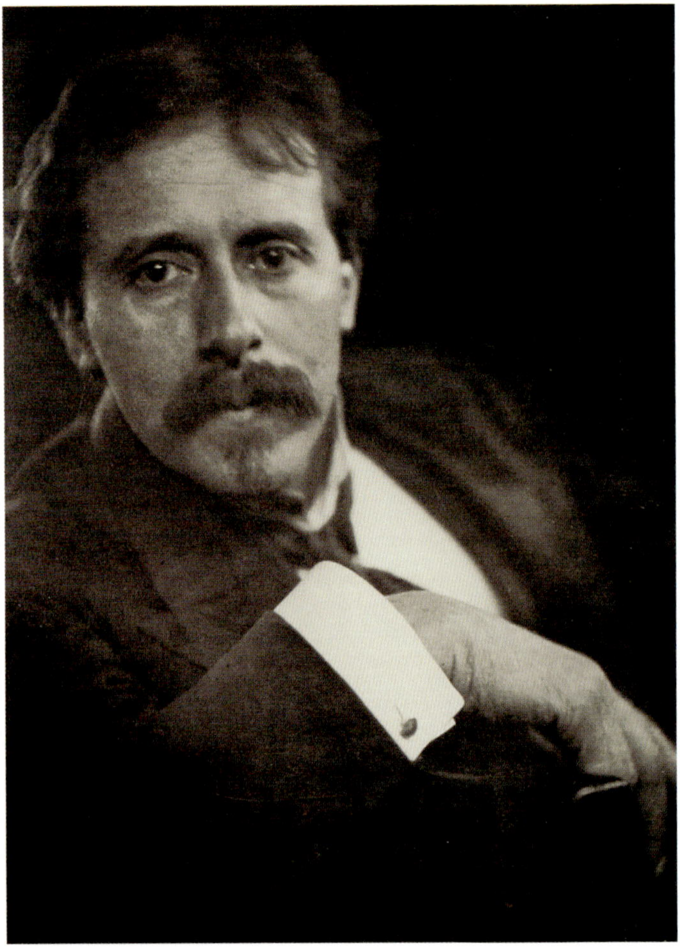

C.R Ashbee photographed by Frank Lloyd Wright while on a visit to Chicago, 1900

C.R Ashbee, Guild of Handicraft green glass decanter with silver mounts, 1901

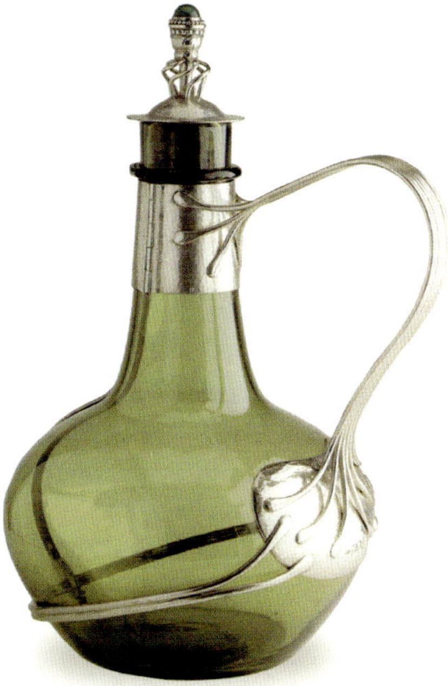

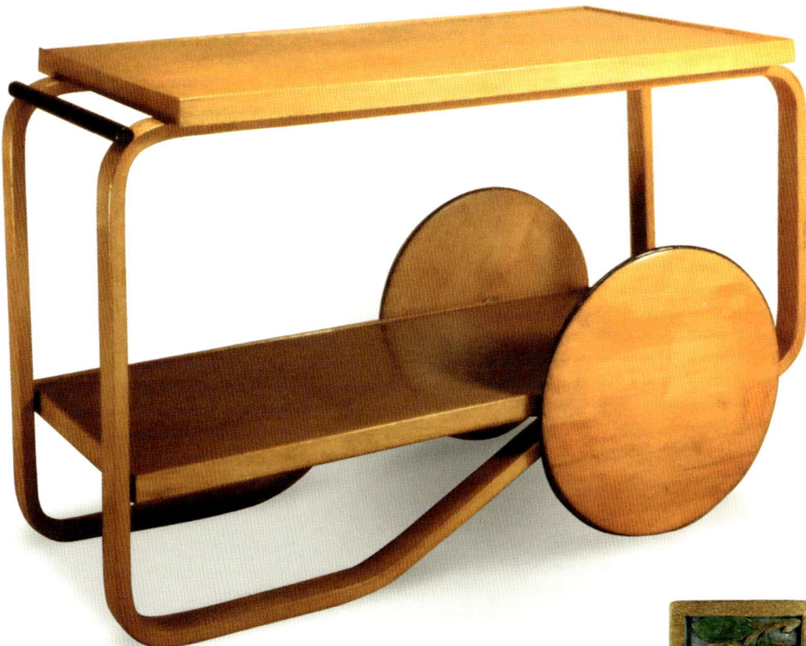

Laminated birch Tea Cart designed by Alvar Aalto, 1936

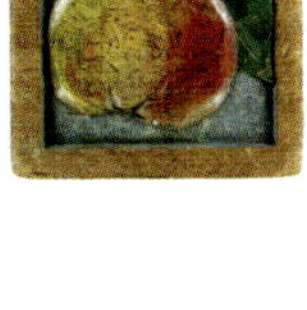

B *is for...* Baillie Scott, Barnsley, Bauhaus, Bayes, Bawden, Behrens, Benson, Bing, Birmingham Guild, Blow, Bodley, Brandt, Brangwyn, Bretby, Breuer, Brewer, Bucknell, Burges, Burmantoft, Burne-Jones & Butterfield.

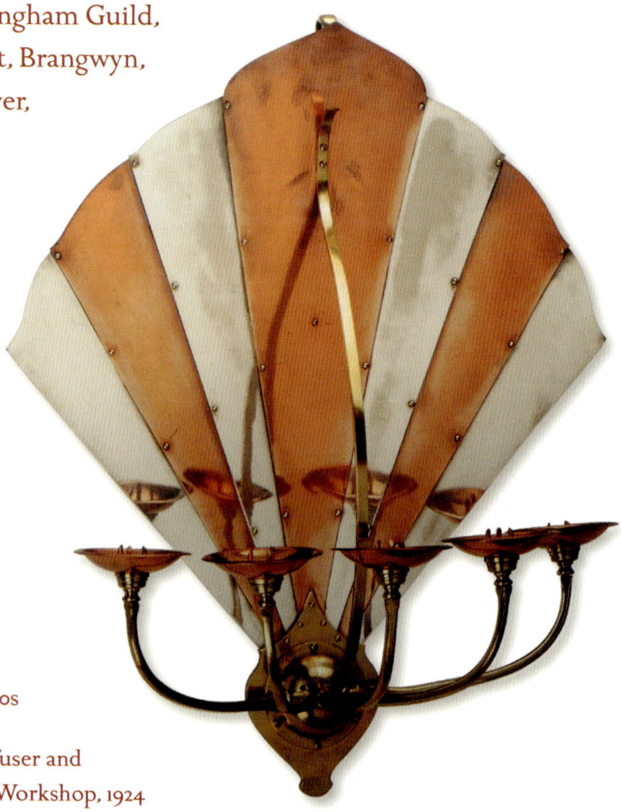

W.A.S. Benson, mixed metal candle sconce, 1890s

Marianne Brandt, tea infuser and strainer, Bauhaus Metal Workshop, 1924

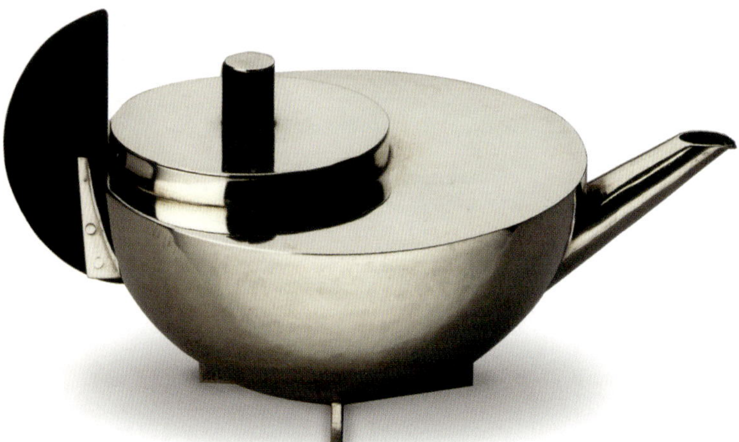

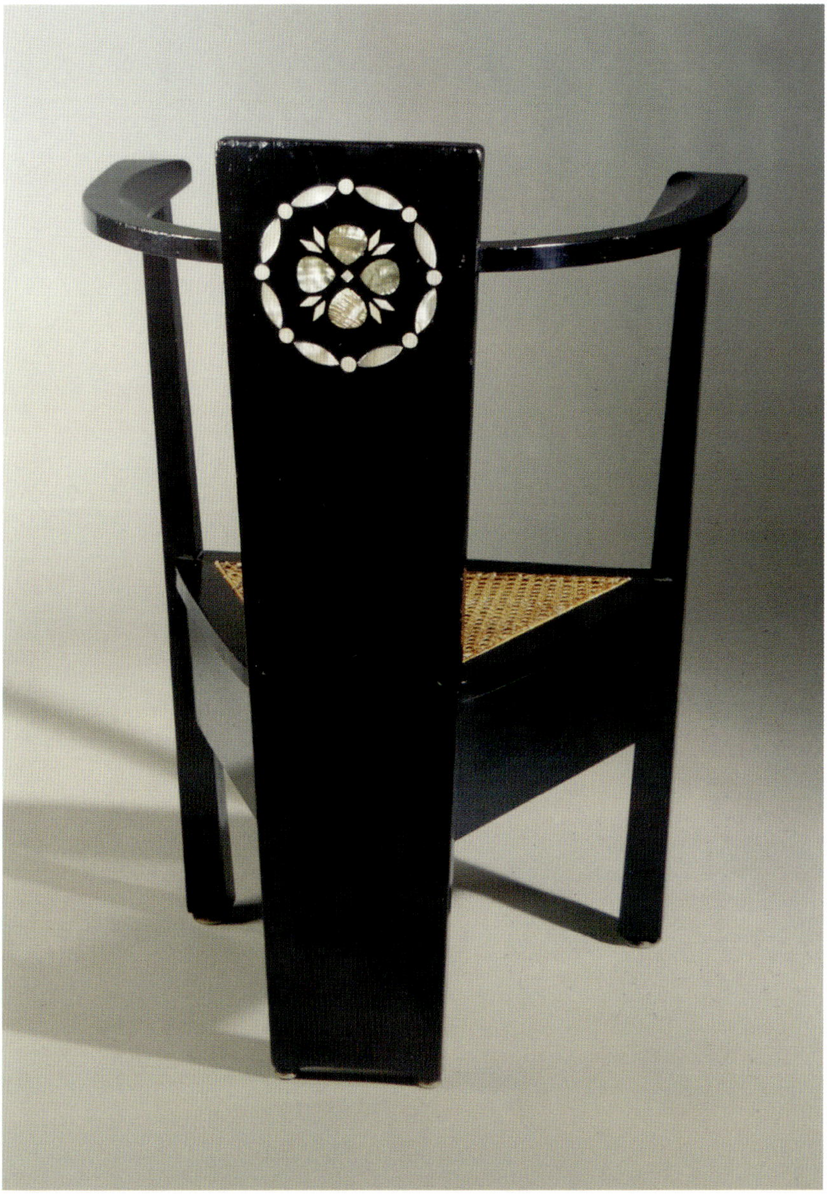

M.H. Baillie Scott, chair ebonised with mother-of-pearl inlay, c.1903. Baille Scott's furniture for the Grand Duke of Hesse, was made by the Guild of Handicraft

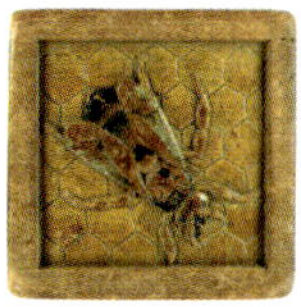

C *is for...* Cardew, Carpenter, Carr, Catterson-Smith, Central School of Arts & Crafts, Century Guild, Clarke, Clausen, Clissett, Cobden-Sanderson, Cockerell, Cole, Cooper, Corbusier, Cranach Press Crane, Creswick, Craig & Cuzner.

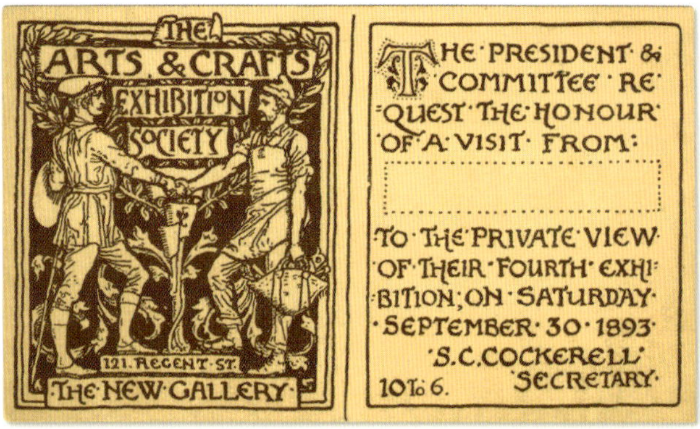

Arts & Crafts Exhibition Society, 1893 invitation designed by Walter Crane

Harry Clarke, independent glass panel, 'Mr Gilhooley', 1929, commissioned by the Irish Government for the League of Nations, Geneva, but never presented

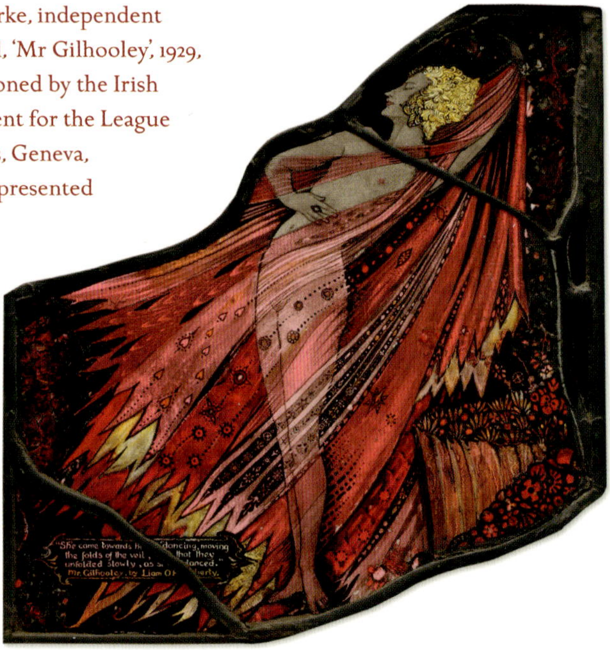

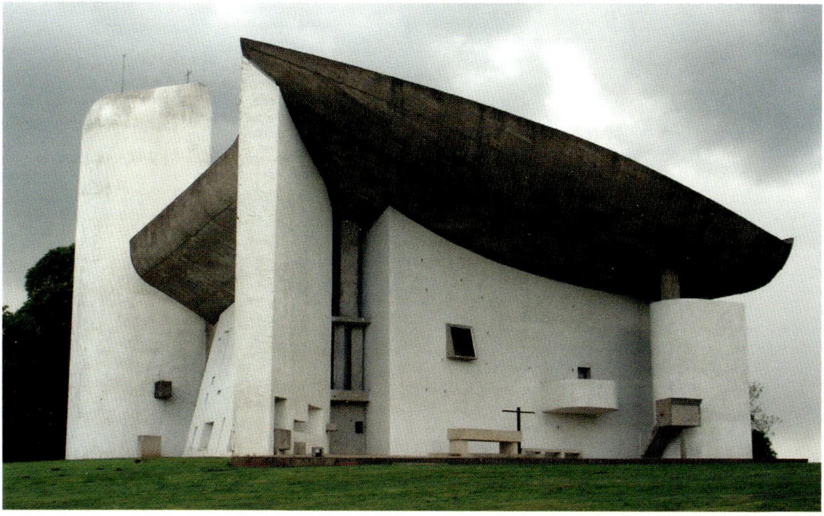

Le Corbusier, Chapel of the Holy Virgin at Ronchamp, 1950–55. Corbusier treated the design as a work of pure sculpture, which has since then often been likened to Noah's ark.

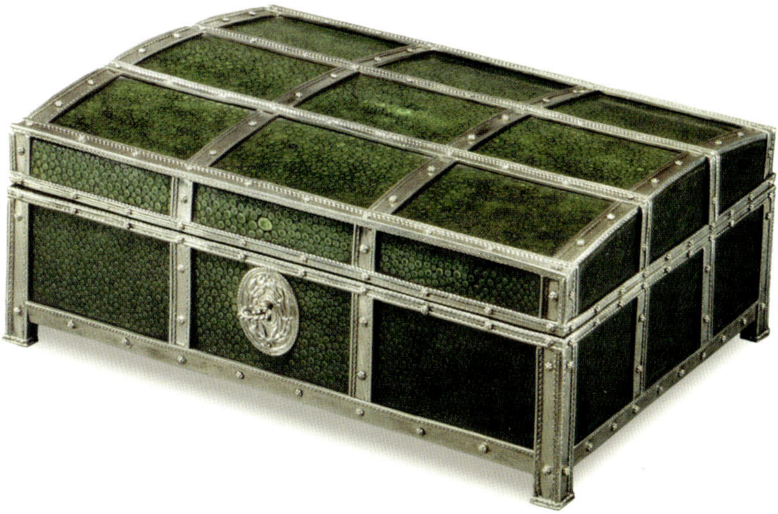

John Paul Cooper, writing box covered in shagreen with silver mounts and strapping, 1903. Cooper, like his friend Henry Wilson, trained as an architect in J.D. Sedding's office

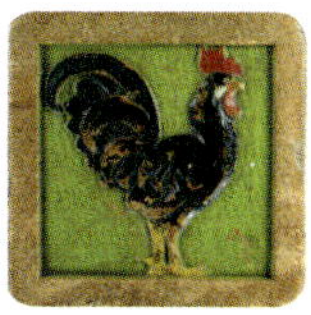

D *is for…* Davoll, Dawson, Day, Dearle, Della Robbia, De Morgan, Design & Industries Association, Deutscher Werkbund, Diaghilev, Dixon, Dolmetsch, Doulton, Doves Press, Dresser, Dressler, Dryad, & Dunbar.

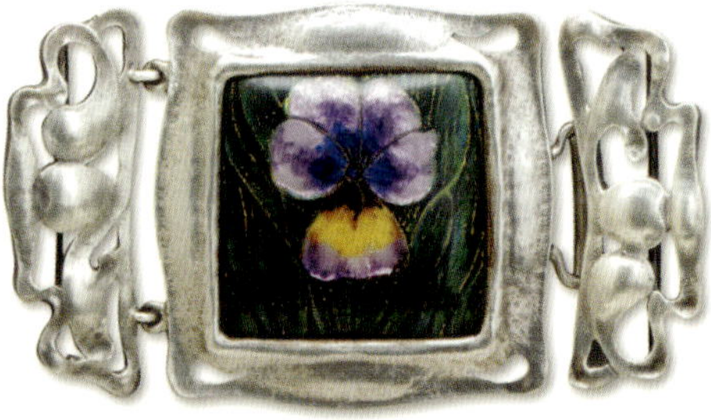

Nelson & Edith Dawson, silver & enamel buckle, c.1905. Edith was a skilled enamellist while her husband did the metalwork

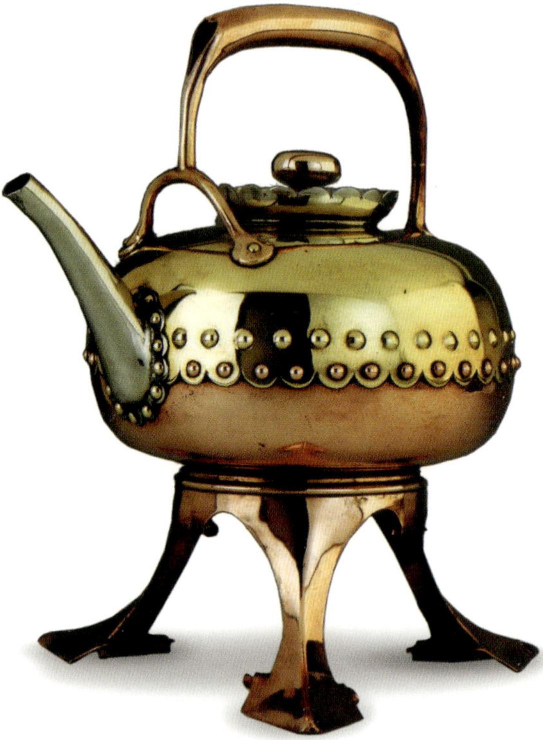

Dr Christopher Dresser, copper and brass kettle and stand made byBenham & Froud, 1880–83

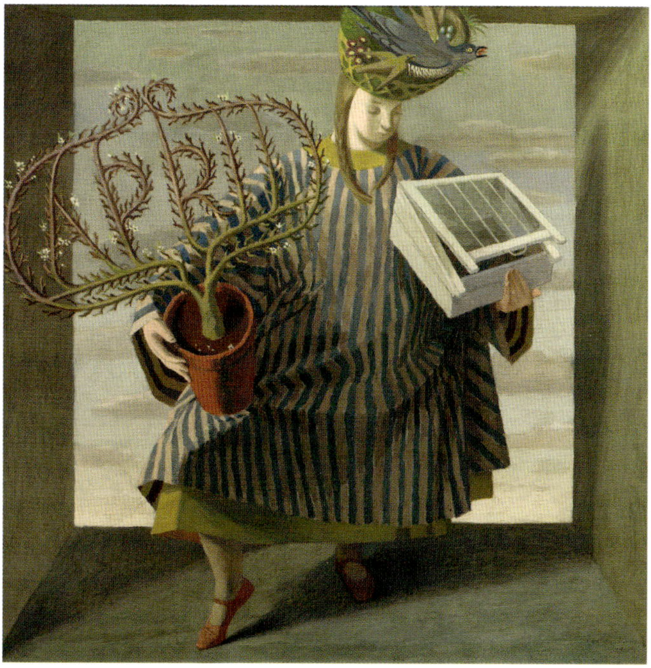

Evelyn Dunbar, *April*, 1937, the design was reused the following year as part of *An English Calendar*

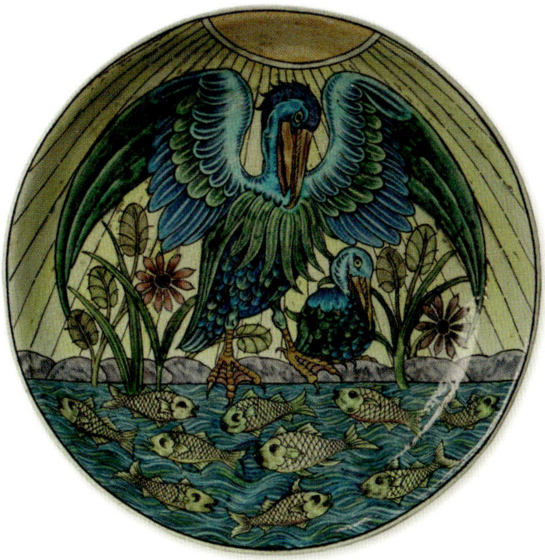

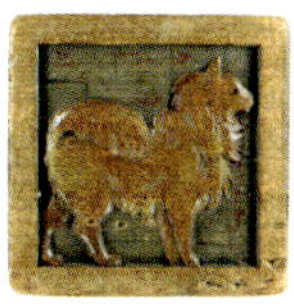

William de Morgan, charger, c.1880. When De Morgan closed his pottery works he hoped that Ashbee might be able to take on some of his men

E *is for...* Eastlake, Eden, Ellis, Elgar, Elmslie, Elton, Emerson, Emanuel, Enamelling, Epstein, Eragny Press, Eriksson, Erotica, Essex House Press, Etchells, Etching & Evans

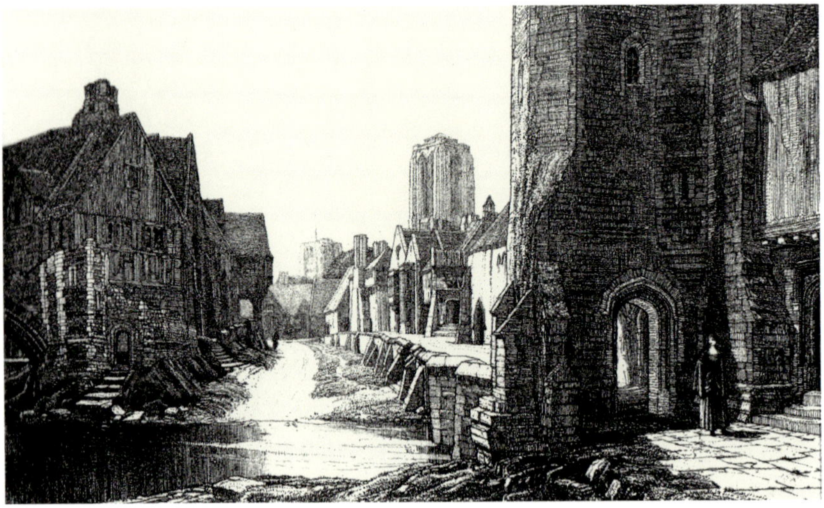

F.L. Griggs, *The Ford*, etching, 1915–24

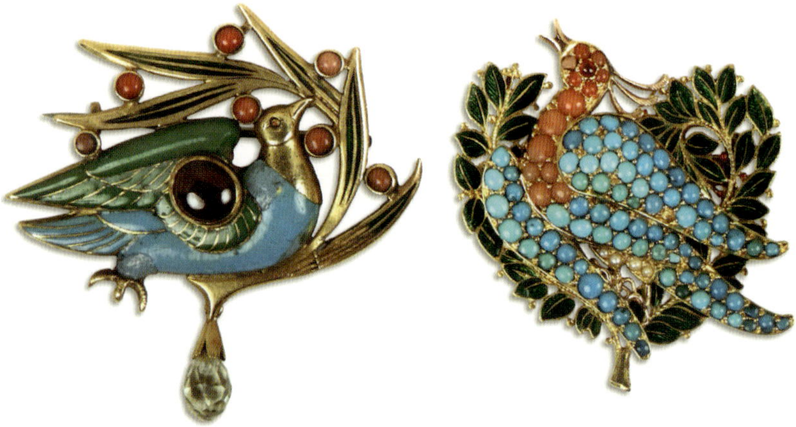

Enameled brooches designed by Charles Ricketts (left) and Burne-Jones (right), made by the Italian jeweller and silversmith, Carlo Giuliano of 115 Piccadilly. Giuliano brought the technique of enamelling to an extraordinary degree of technical perfection

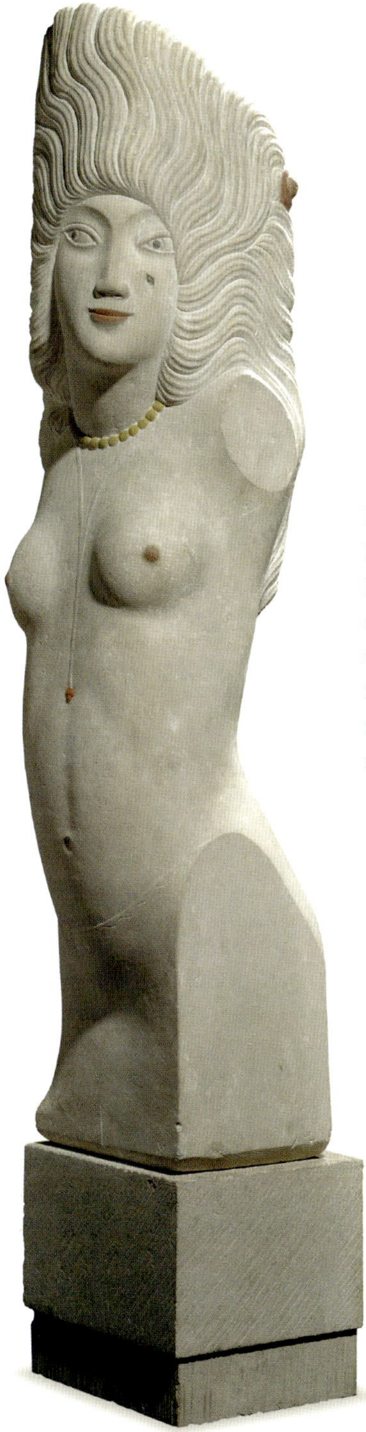

Eric Gill, *The Headdress,* Beer stone, 1928. Gill heightened the erotic quality of this torso with touches of red paint, including the extra rose-bud nipple in the model's hair

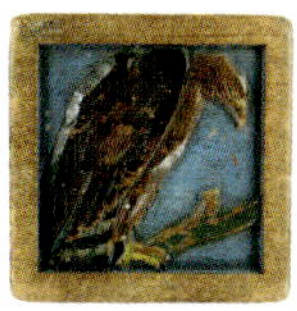

F *is for…*
Faulkner,
Falkirk Iron Co.,
Fehr, Finberg,
Finch, Fisher, Fletcher,
Foley, Forbes, Ford,
Fors Clavigera, Forsyth,
Frampton, Frith & Fry

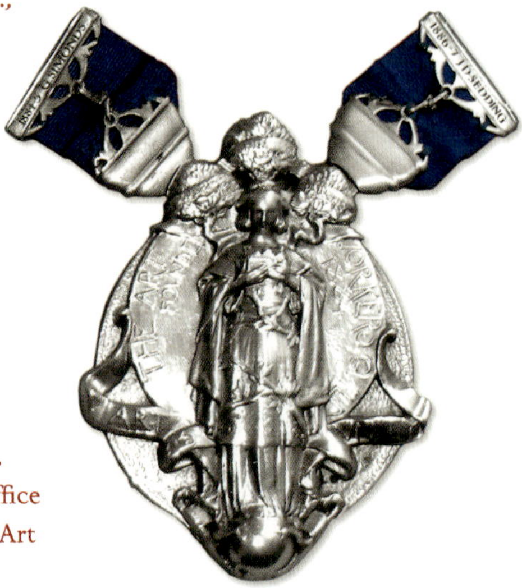

Sir George Frampton,
badge and chain of office
for the Master of the Art
Workers' Guild, 1902

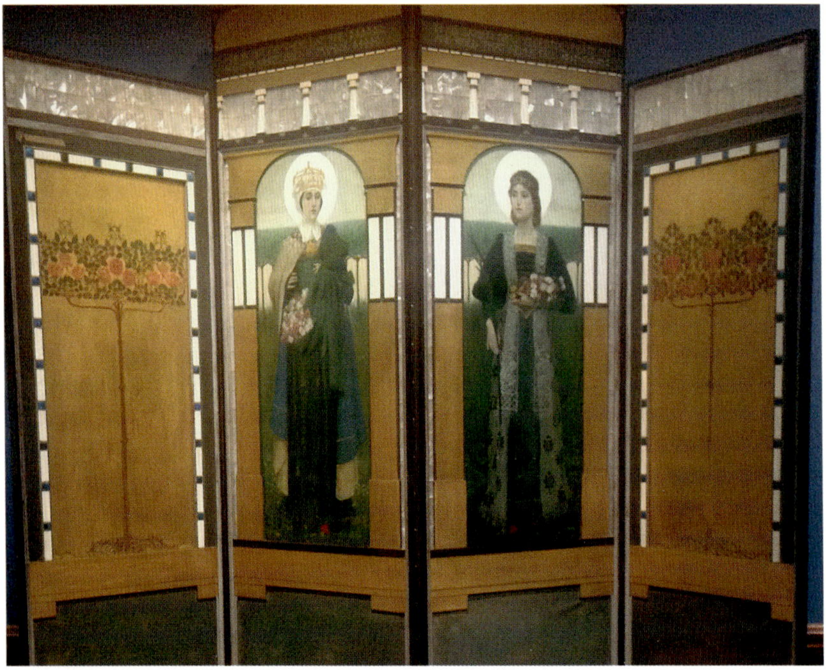

Decorative screen, Sir George Frampton, 1890s

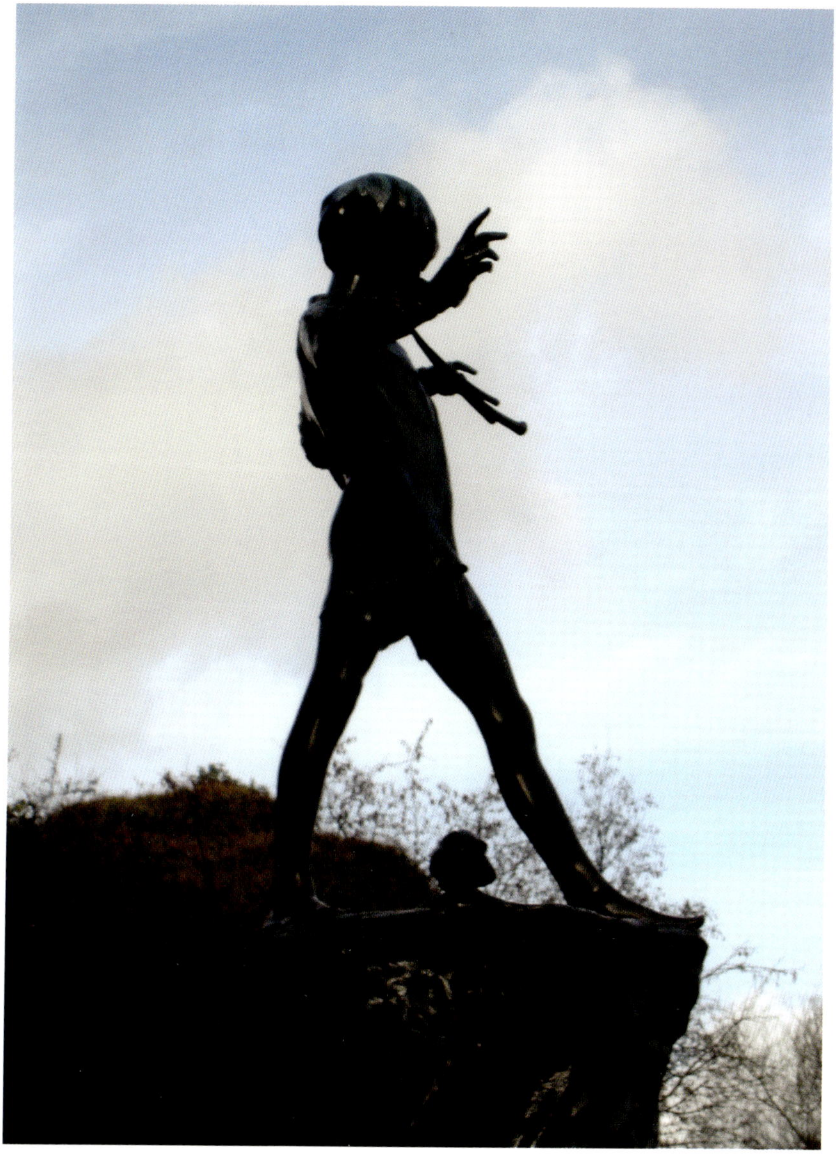

Sir George Frampton was one of the most multi-talented craftsmen of his generation, excelling in the decorative arts, but is primarily known as a sculptor. The statue of Nurse Edith Cavell in St. Martin's Place, Trafalgar Square and Peter Pan (1911–12) being two of the best known.

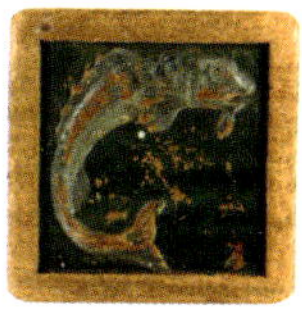

G *is for...* Gallé, Gamble, Gaskin, Geddes, Gere, Gilbert, Gill, Gimson, Giuliano, Glasgow School, Godwin, Grainger, Greene & Greene, Griffin, Griggs, Gropius, Grueby, Guild of Handicraft & Guild of St George

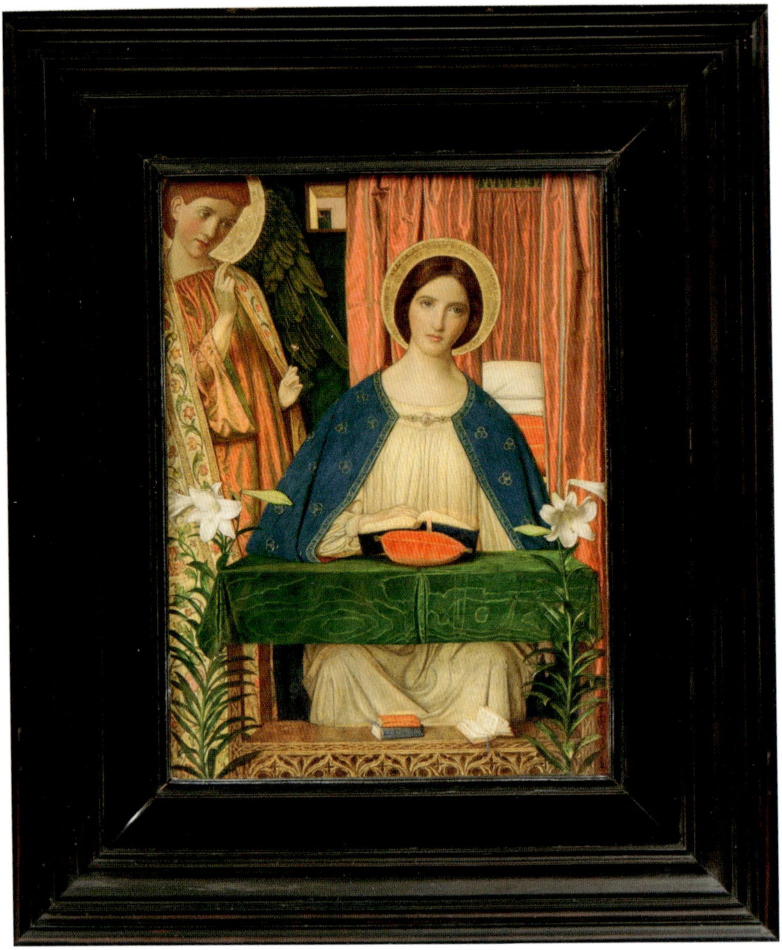

Arthur Gaskin, *The Annunciation*, 1898. Gaskin was headmaster of Birmingham's Vittoria Street School, and played a major role in the tempera revival, as well as collaborating with his wife, Georgie, in the production of a wide range of metalwork and jewellery.

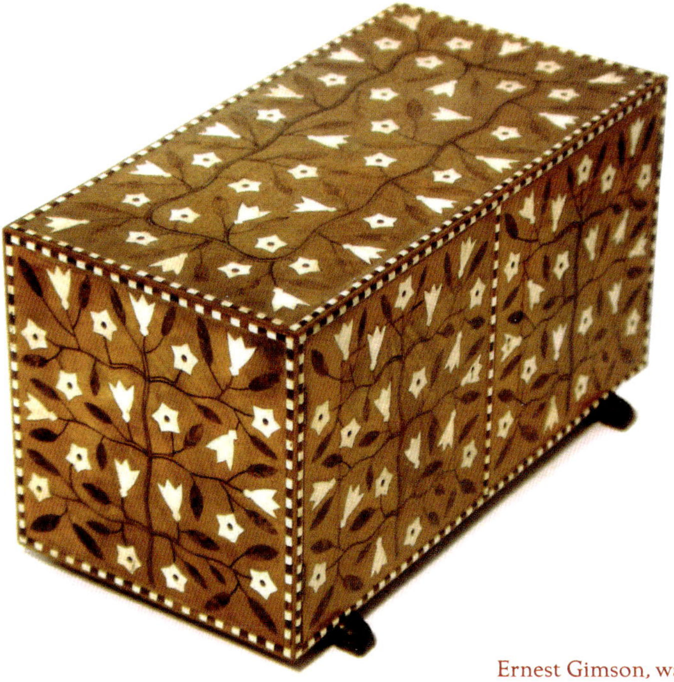

Ernest Gimson, walnut casket inlaid with ebony and ivory, c.1905

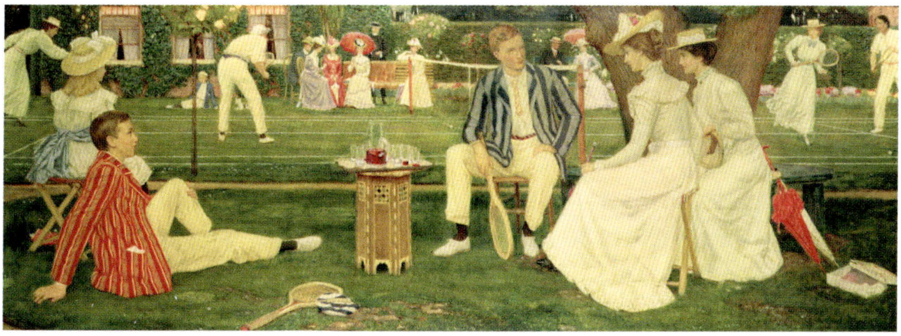

Charles March Gere, *The Tennis Party*, 1900, shows the Birmingham artist-craftsman at play. Gere's sister Margaret is depicted top left, while his other sister, Edith, is playing tennis with her husband Henry Payne top right

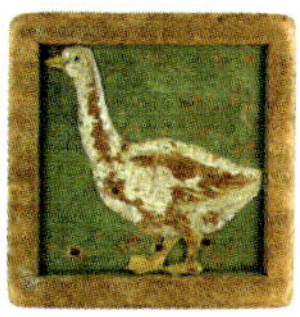

H *is for...* Hamada, Hardman, Hart, Haseler, Heal & Sons, Heaton, Herter, Hesse, *Hobby Horse*, Hoffmann, Holden, Holiday, Hollyer, Holst, Home Arts & Industries Association, Horne, Housman, Hubbard & Hukin & Heath.

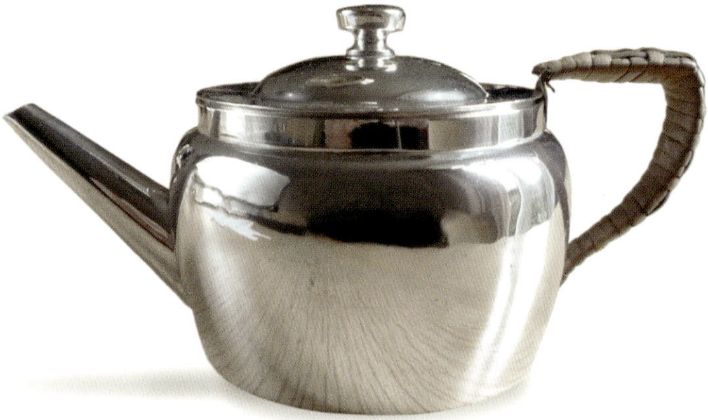

Hukin & Heath silver teapot hallmarked Birmingham, 1879 (above) and (below) electroplated letter or toastrack 1881 also manufactured by Hukin & Heath, both designed by Dr. Christopher Dresser

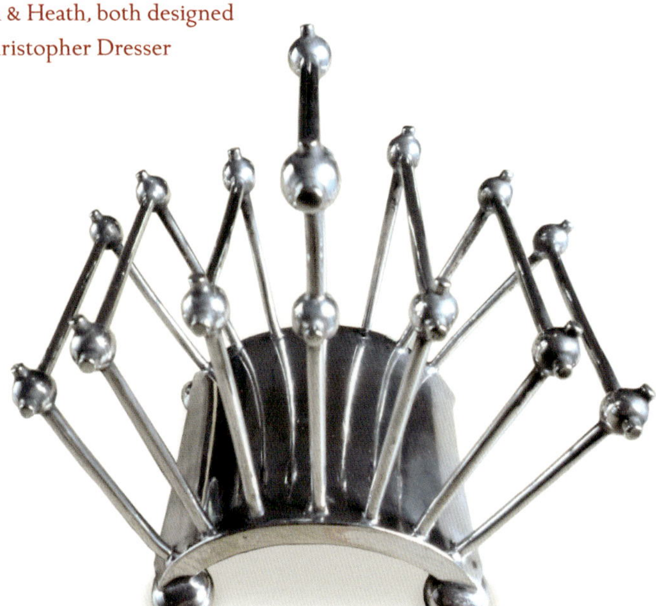

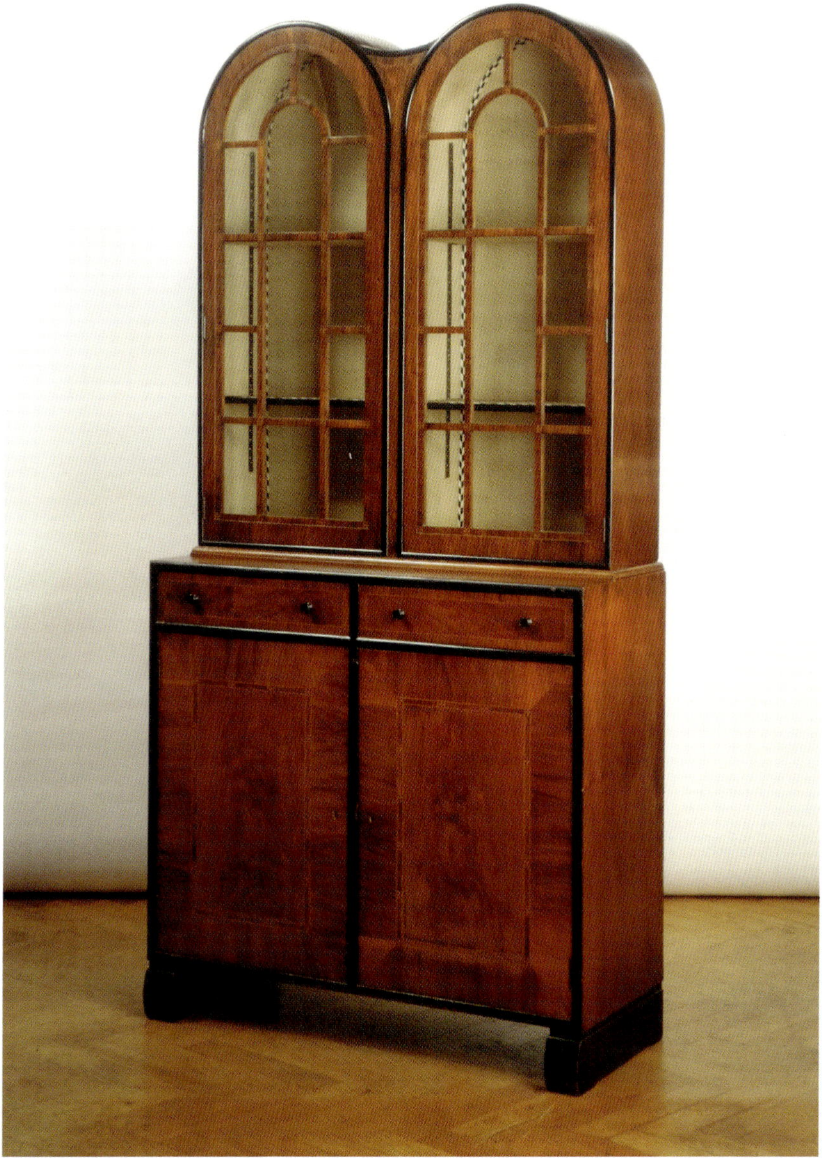

Heal & Son double dome cabinet in walnut, c.1923. The firm of Heal's was established in Tottenham Court Road as 'mattress & featherbed manufacturers' as early as 1818. It was transformed in the early 20th-century by (Sir) Ambrose Heal, who joined as a trainee in 1895

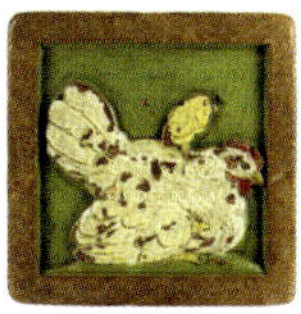

I *is for...* Iles, Illumination, Image, Ionides, Irish Home Industries Association, Ironwork, Irving & Ivory work

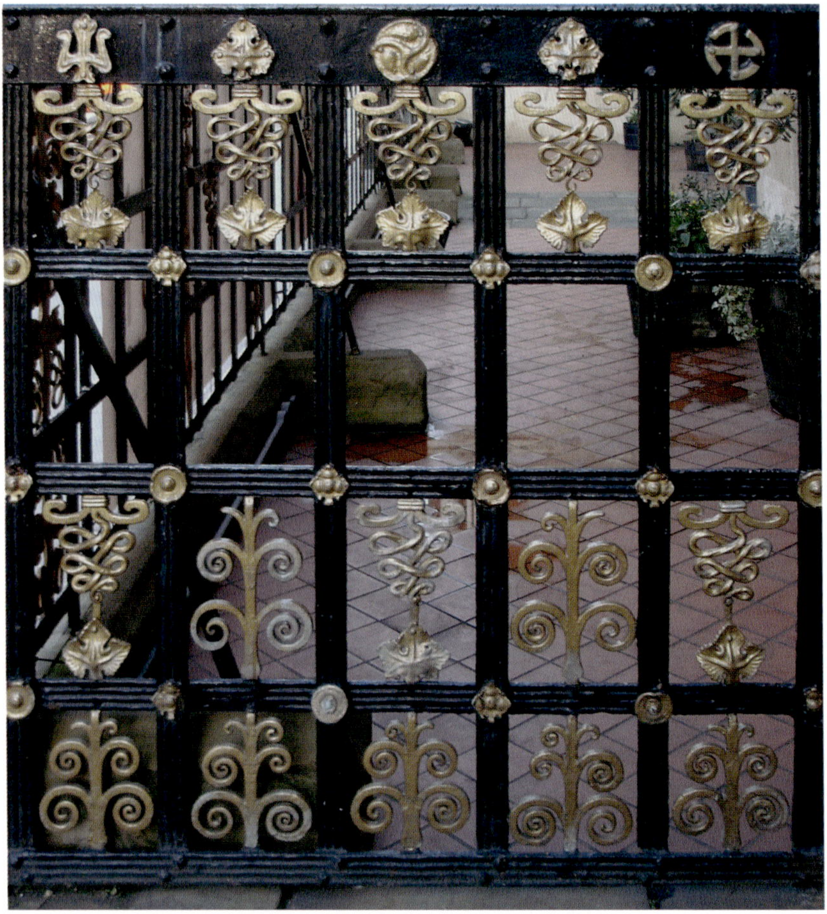

Ironwork gates and railings to Holy Trinity, Sloane Street, London, designed by Henry Wilson, 1902

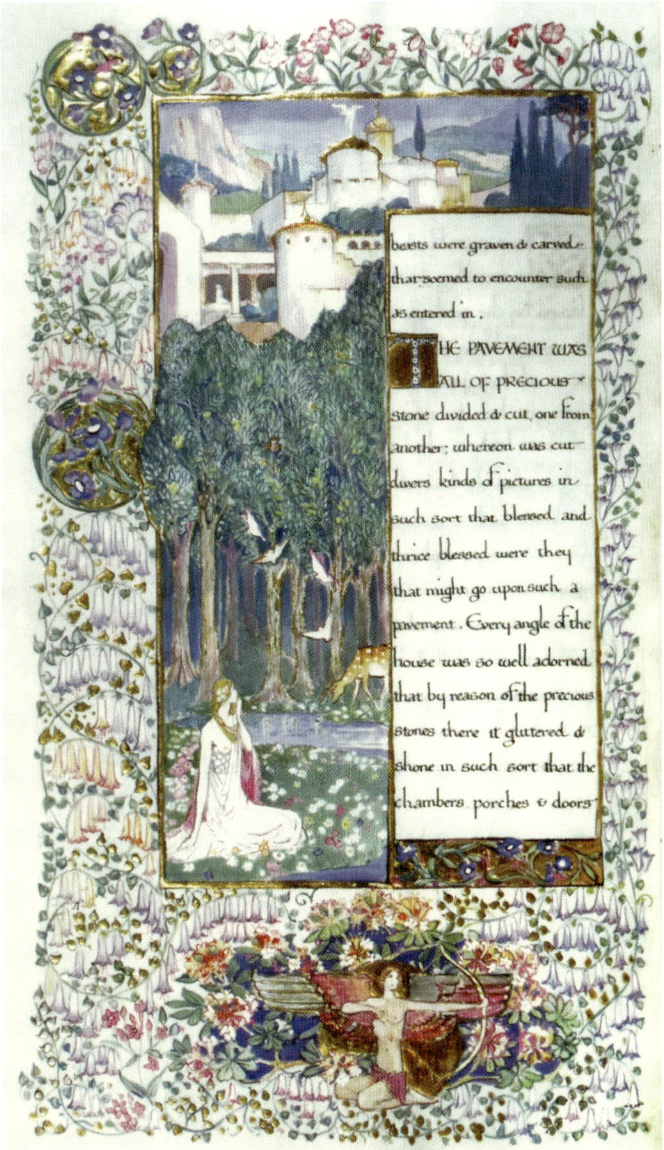

Page from an illuminated manuscript by Jessie Bayes, 1920s. The Bayes family were important contributors to the Arts and Crafts. Jessie's brother Gilbert was a renowned sculptor, who also designed for Doulton's, while Walter Bayes was a painter exhibiting with Sickert and the Camden Town Group.

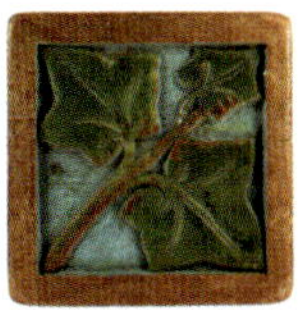

J *is for...* Jack, Jackson, Jacomb-Hood, Jeanneret, Jeffrey & Co, Jeckyll, Jensen, Jewellery, Jewson, Joass, John, Johnston, Jones & Jowett.

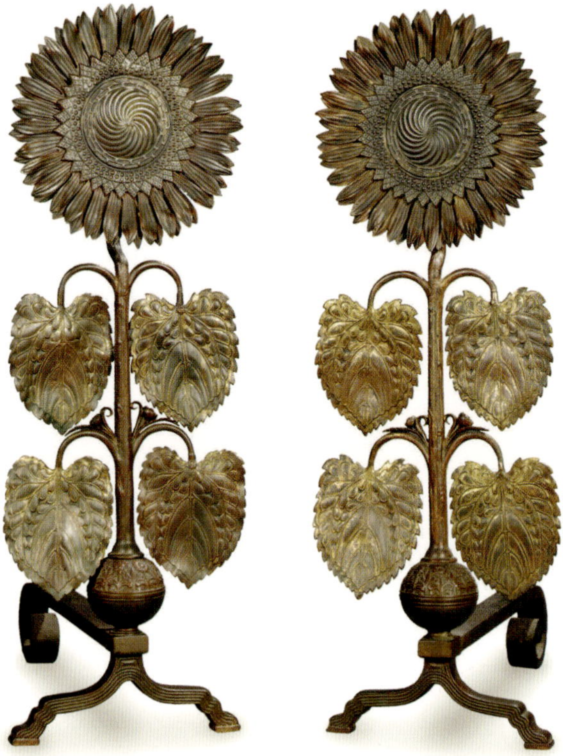

Pair of sunflower firedogs designed by Thomas Jeckyll and made by Barnard, Bishop & Barnard, c.1870

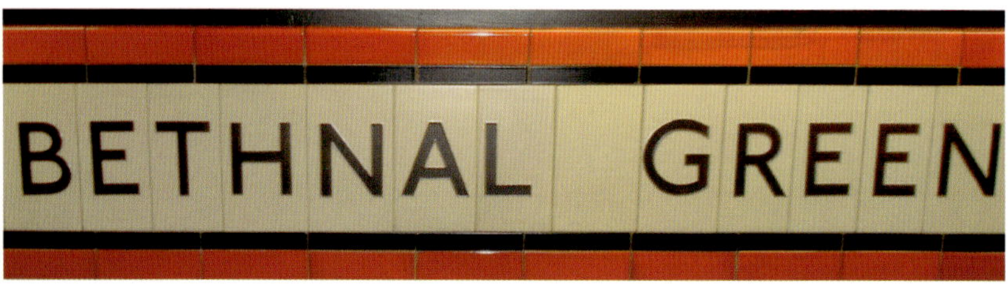

Edward Johnston's sans serif letter form devised for the London Underground, 1916

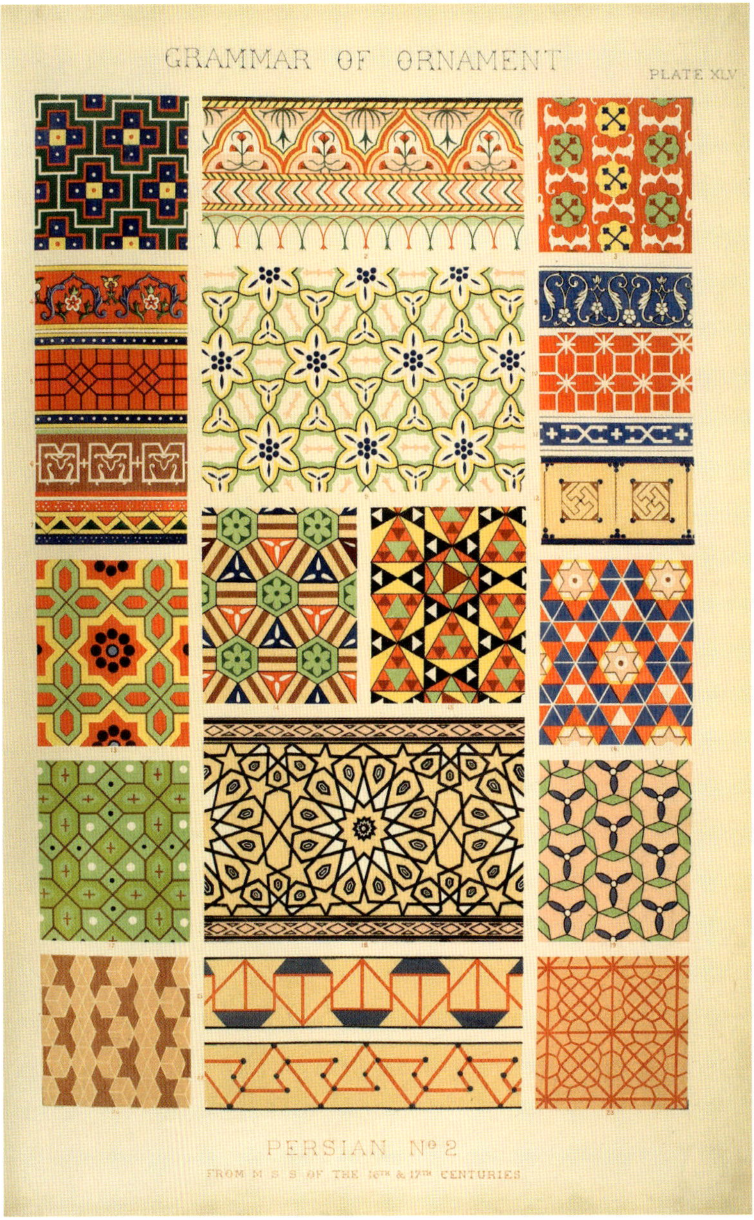

Page from Owen Jones's *Grammar of Ornament*, 1856. Jones had originally studied the Islamic decoration at the Alhambra in Granada. He became the most influential design theorist of the 19th century

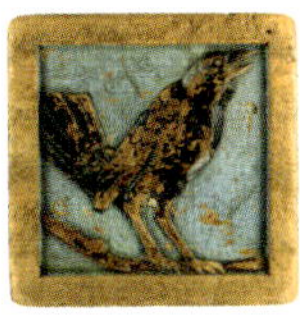

K *is for...* Karl Marx, Kelmscott Press, Kenton & Co, Kessler, Keswick School of Industrial Design, King, Kipling, Kipp, Klimt, Knox, Koizumi, Korovin, Kokoschka & Krall.

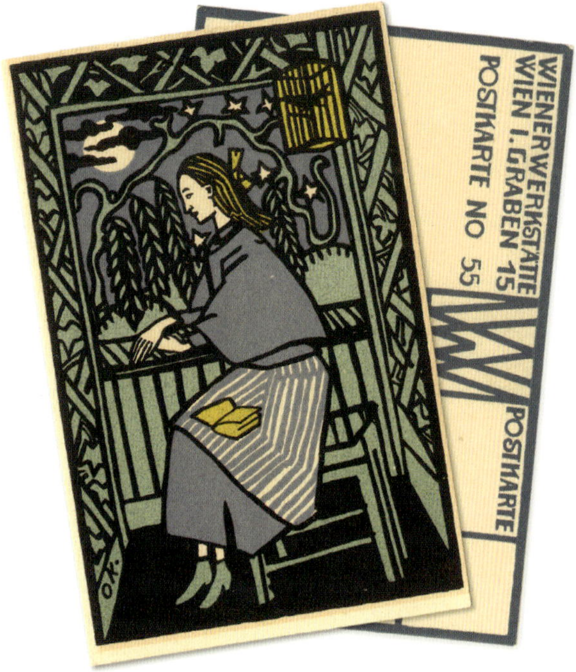

Oskar Kokoschka *Girl at the Window* postcard, the Vienna Werkstatte symbol and address are printed on the reverse, 1907

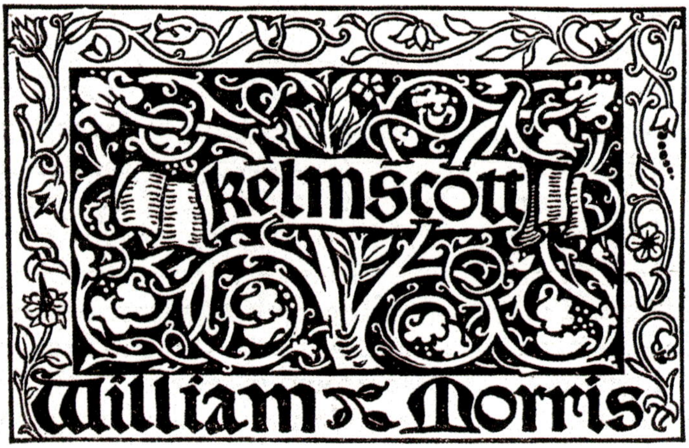

First colophon designed by William Morris for his Kelmscott Press, c.1890

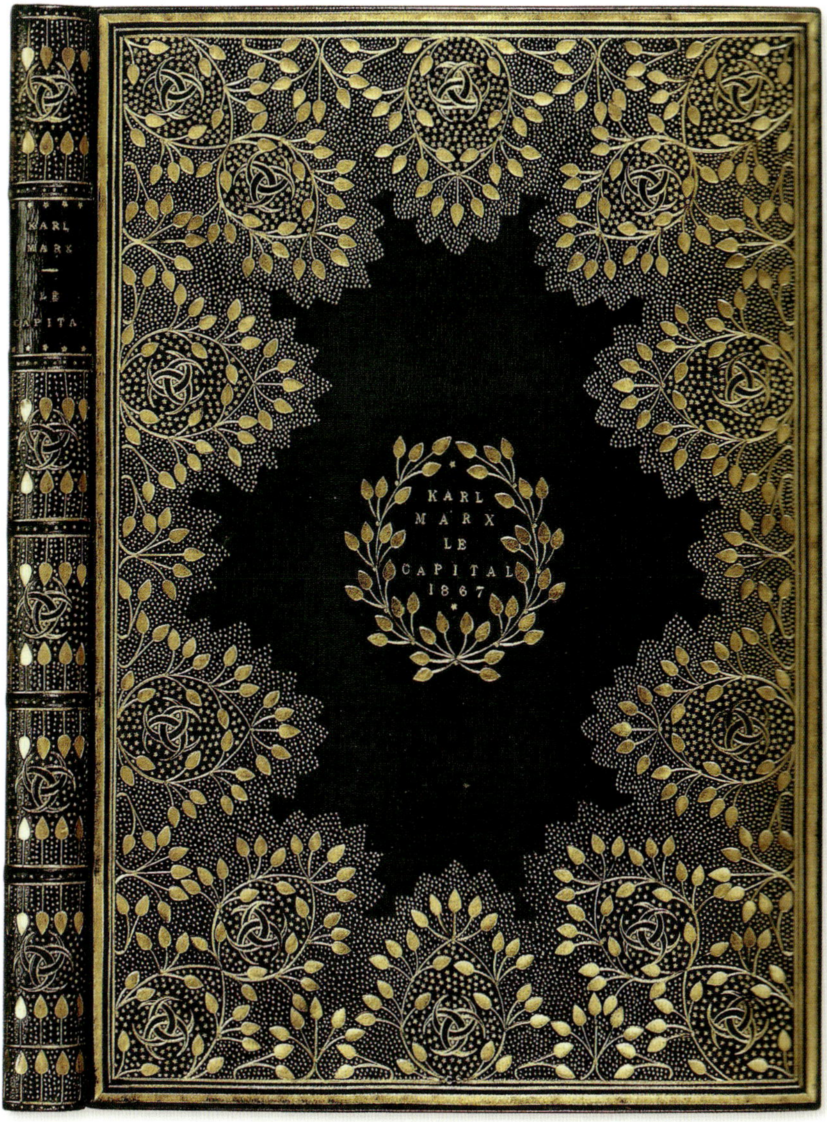

T.J. Cobden-Sanderson's elaborately tooled binding, 1884, for William Morris's copy of Karl Marx's *Le Capital*, 1867

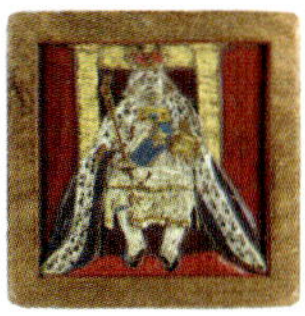

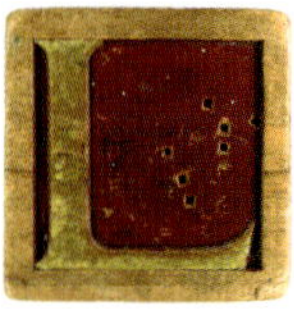

is for... Labelling, La Farge, Lambeth School of Art, Larsson, Leach, Lee, Leighton, Lethaby, Lewis, Liberty & Co, Lighting, Linthorpe, Longden, Loos, Lorimer, Lovat Fraser, Lowndes & Lutyens.

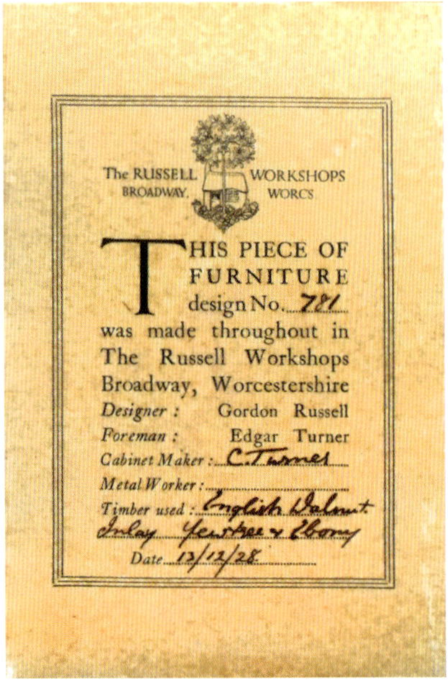
The RUSSELL WORKSHOPS
BROADWAY. WORCS

THIS PIECE OF FURNITURE design No. 781 was made throughout in The Russell Workshops Broadway, Worcestershire

Designer : Gordon Russell
Foreman : Edgar Turner
Cabinet Maker : C. Turner
Metal Worker :
Timber used : English Walnut Inlay Yewtree & Ebony
Date 12/12/28

A typical trade label from the Gordon Russell Workshops, Broadway, Worcestershire 1928, detailing design number, craftsman, materials and date of completion of work

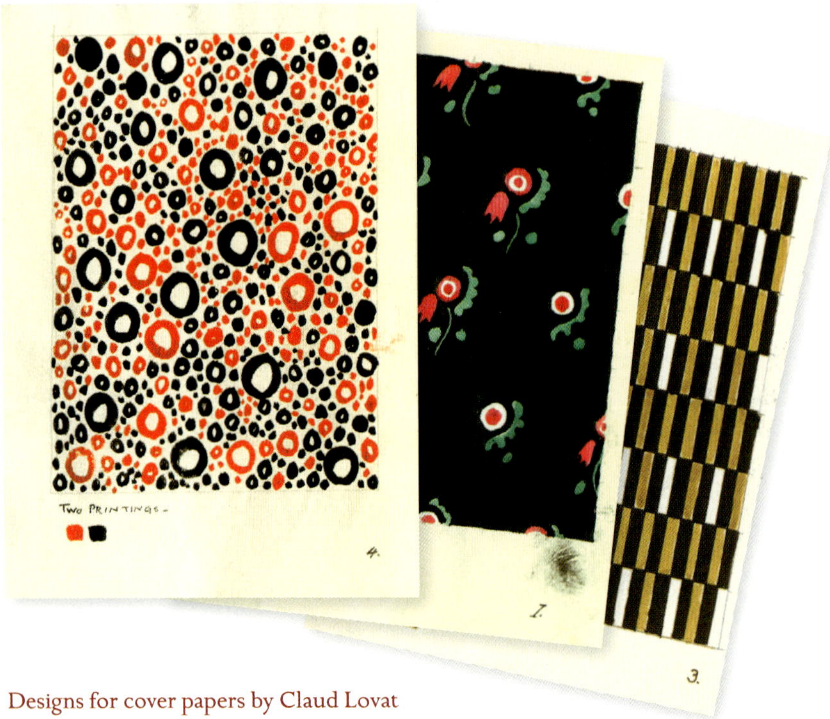

Designs for cover papers by Claud Lovat Fraser, 1920, some of these were also adapted for textiles for Liberty & Co

Light fitting designed by Sir Edwin Lutyens for the Imperial bungalows, New Delhi, c.1920

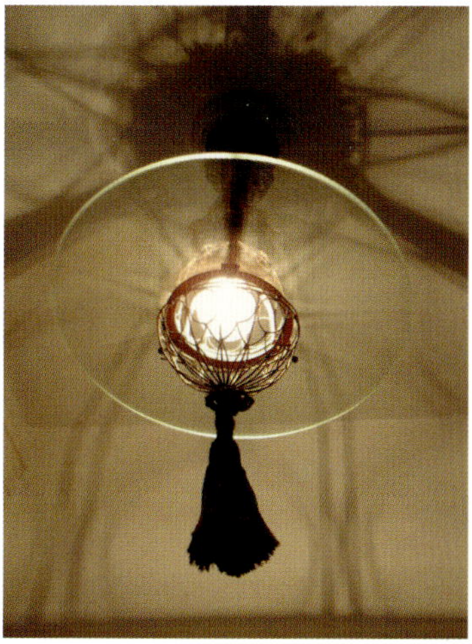

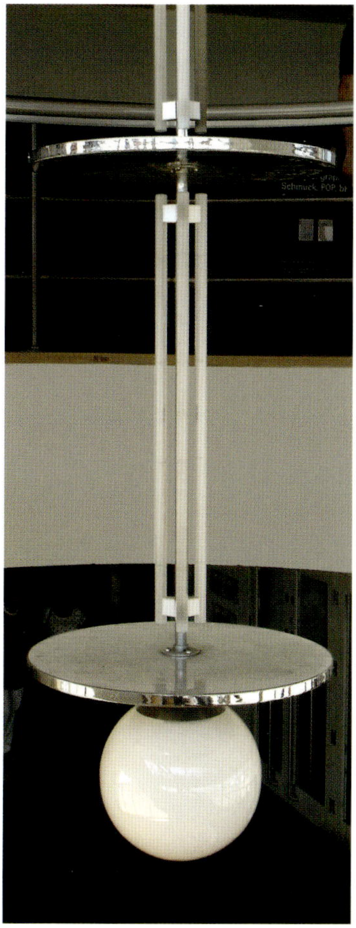

Hanging light designed by Erich Mendelsohn for the De La Warr Pavilion, Bexhill, c.1935

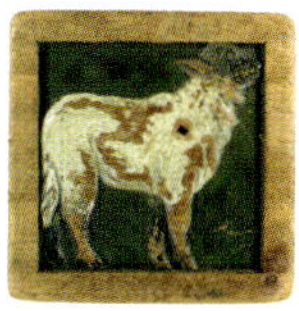

M *is for...* Macdonald, Mackintosh, Mackmurdo, MacNair, McKim, Maher, Mairet, Mamontov, Marblehead, Marshall, Martin, Maybeck, Mead, Meiji, Merton Abbey, Meteyard, Miller, Morris, Morton, Moser, Mucha, Munthe, & Muthesius.

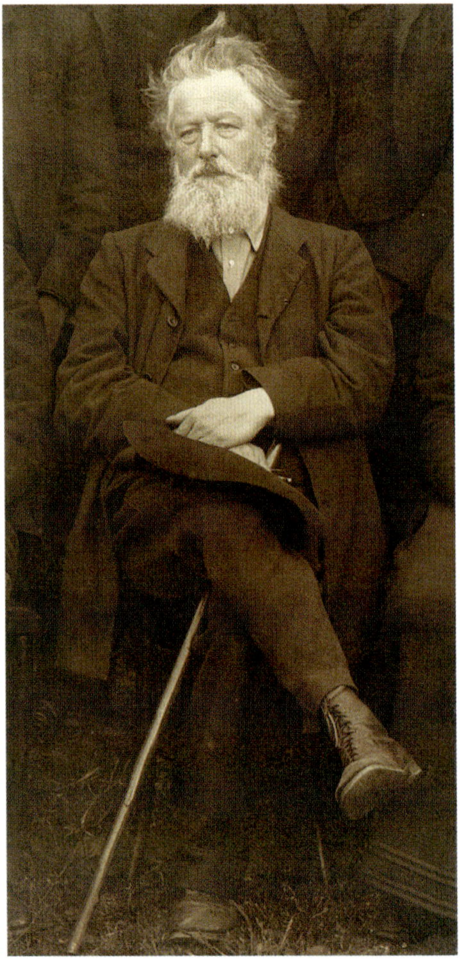

William Morris on the Kelmscott Press 'wayzgoose', 13 September 1895, hand tinted photograph by Emery Walker

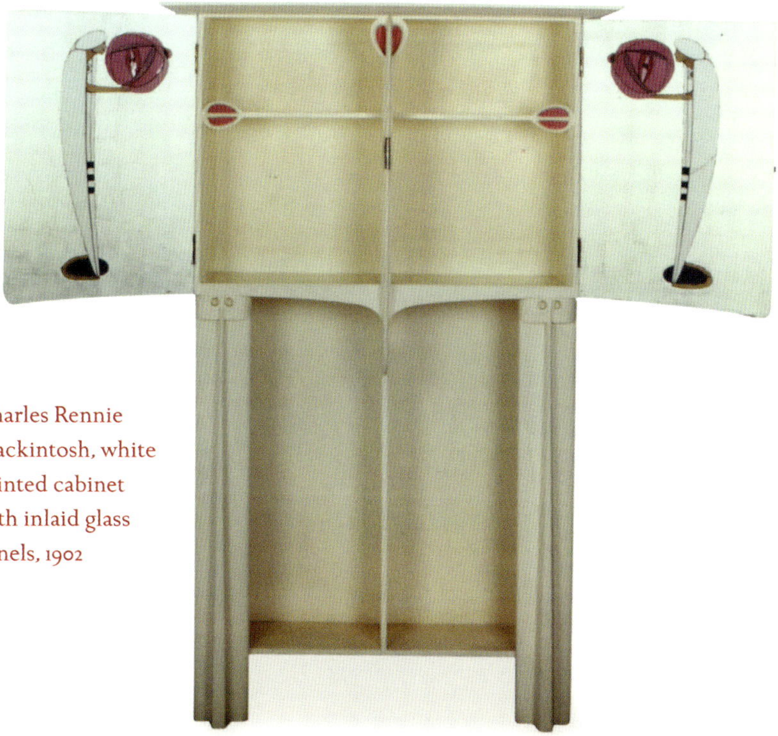

Charles Rennie Mackintosh, white painted cabinet with inlaid glass panels, 1902

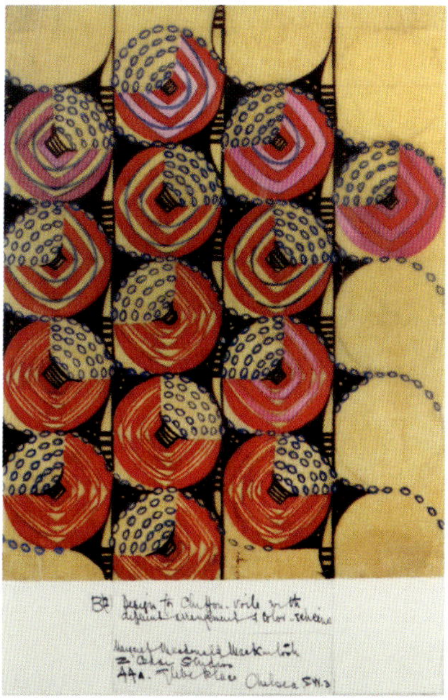

Margaret Macdonald Mackintosh, design for chiffon voile showing different arrangement and colour schemes

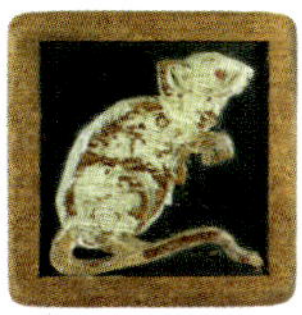

N *is for...* Nash, Neatby, Necklace, Nelson, New, Newbery, Newill, Newlyn School, Newill, Nicholson Nielsen, Nixon, Nonesuch Press & Nuttgens.

Paul Nash, *St Pancras,* Nash's first wood engraving, 1919. A view from his flat across the Euston Road.

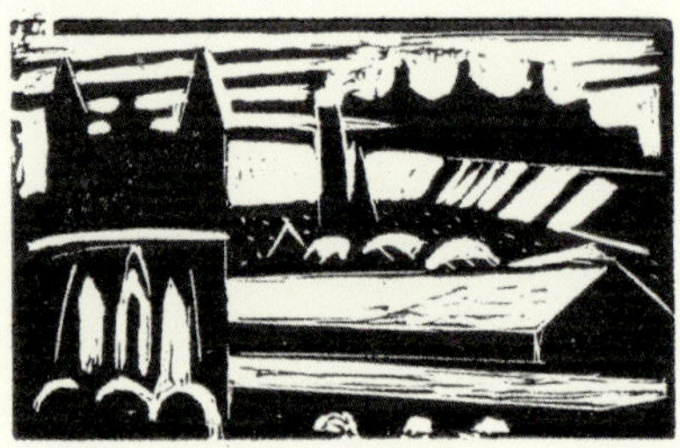

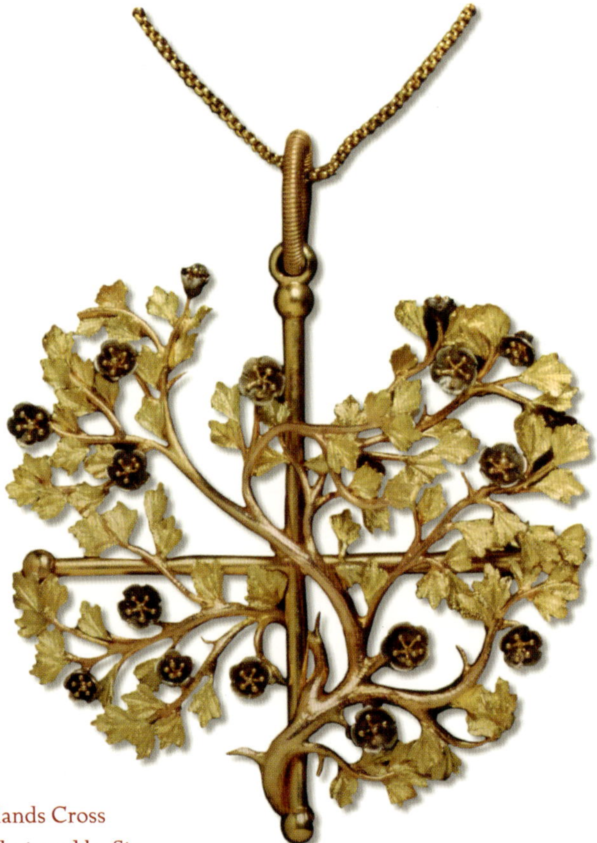

The Whitelands Cross and chain, designed by Sir Edward Burne-Jones for John Ruskin, 1883

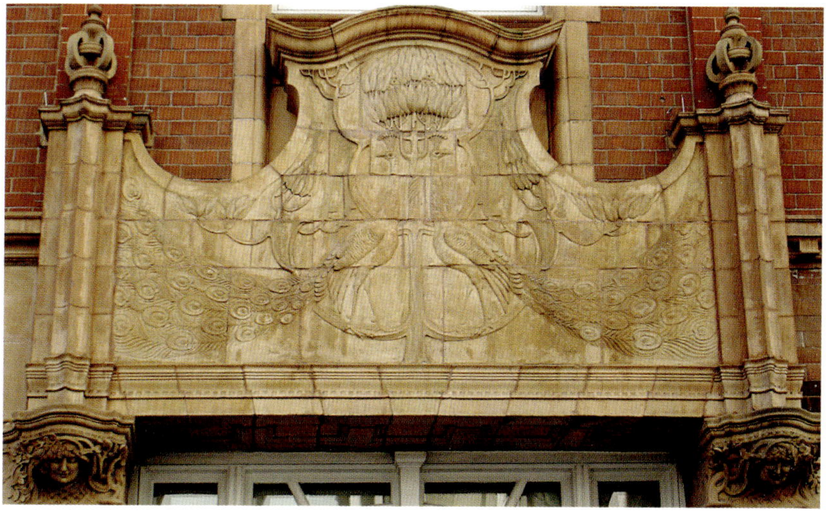

Terracotta panel designed by W.J. Neatby and manufactured by Doulton's for the facade of a building in Great Smith Street, Westminster

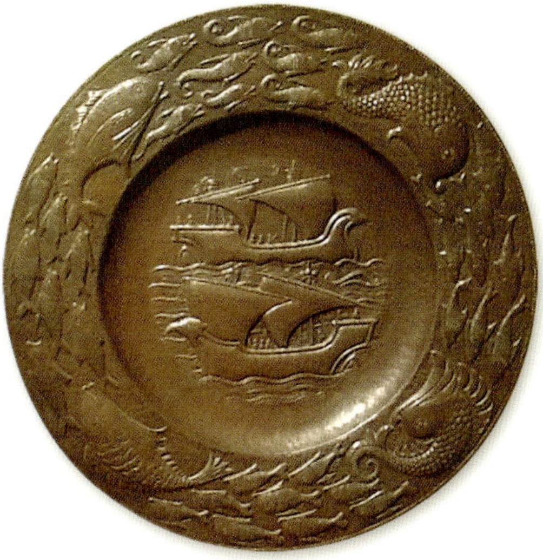

Newlyn School beaten copper charger designed by John Pearson, c.1905. Pearson was the senior metal worker with the Guild of Handicraft at Toynbee Hall, but resigned in 1892 before moving to Cornwall

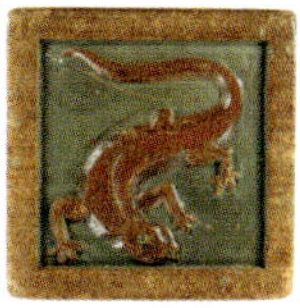

O *is for...* Obrist, Okey, Olbrich, Oliver, Olivier, Omega Workshops, Ornamental, Orrefors, Osborne & Owen

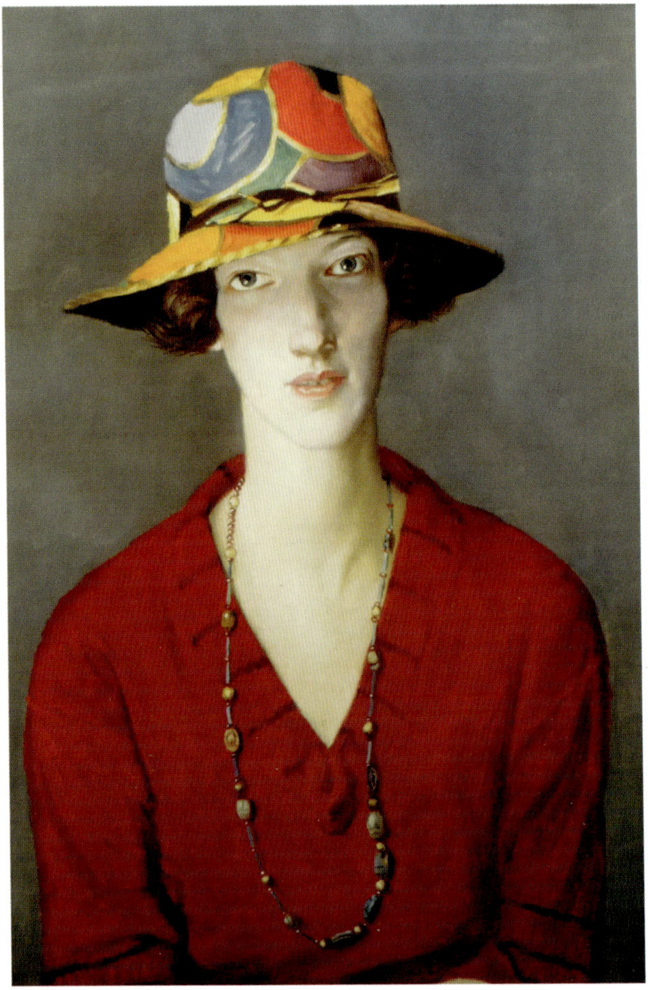

William Strang, *The Jazz Hat*, 1920, both the hat and the long necklace with painted Poole-ware beads are products of the Omega Workshops

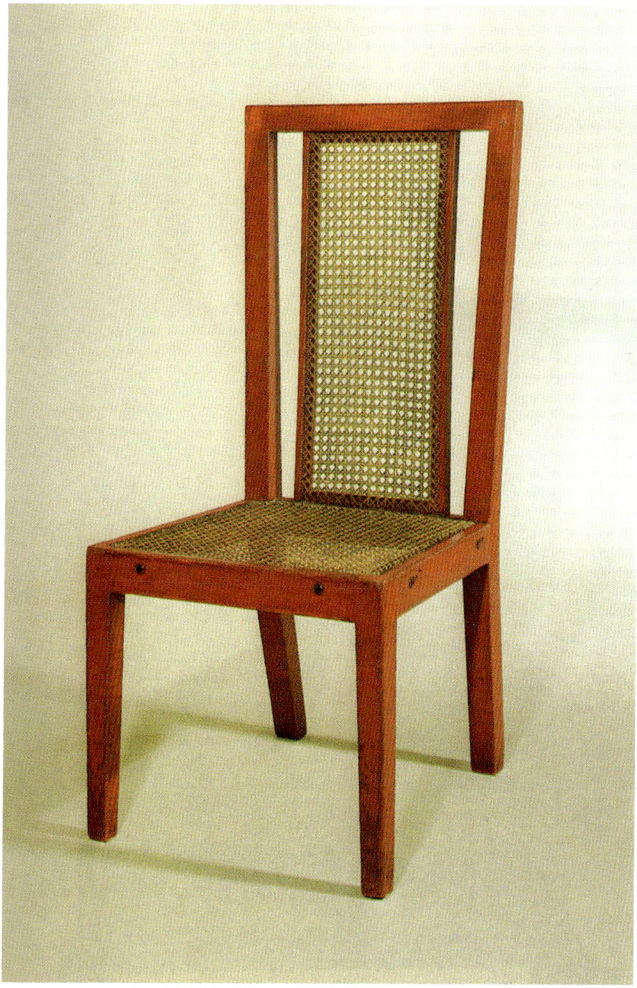

Red painted Omega Workshops dining chair, c.1913, designed by Roger Fry, a close friend of Ashbee's from their student days at King's College, Cambridge. In 1893 he painted a mural for the Magpie and Stump, Ashbee's house in Cheyne Walk, Chelsea

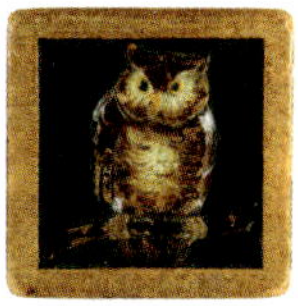

P *is for...* Parker, Partridge, Passenger, Payne, Pearson, Pevsner, Pick, Pilkington, Piper, Pissarro, Pite, Plunkett, Poiret, Pollen, Poole, Pomeroy, Powell, Prairie School, Prior, Pryde, Pugin & Pyghtle Works

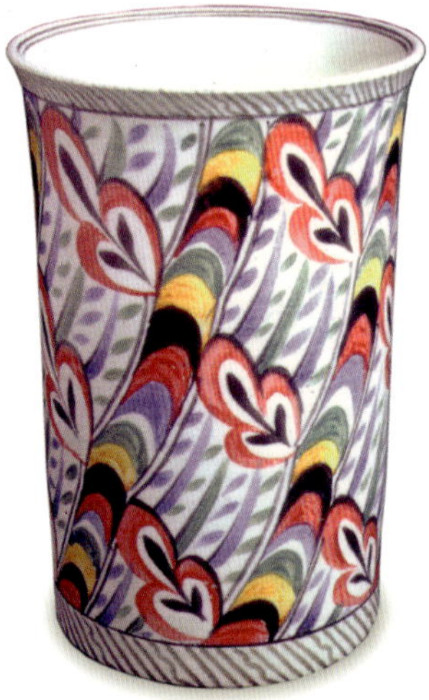

Wedgwood vase decorated by Louise Powell, c.1930

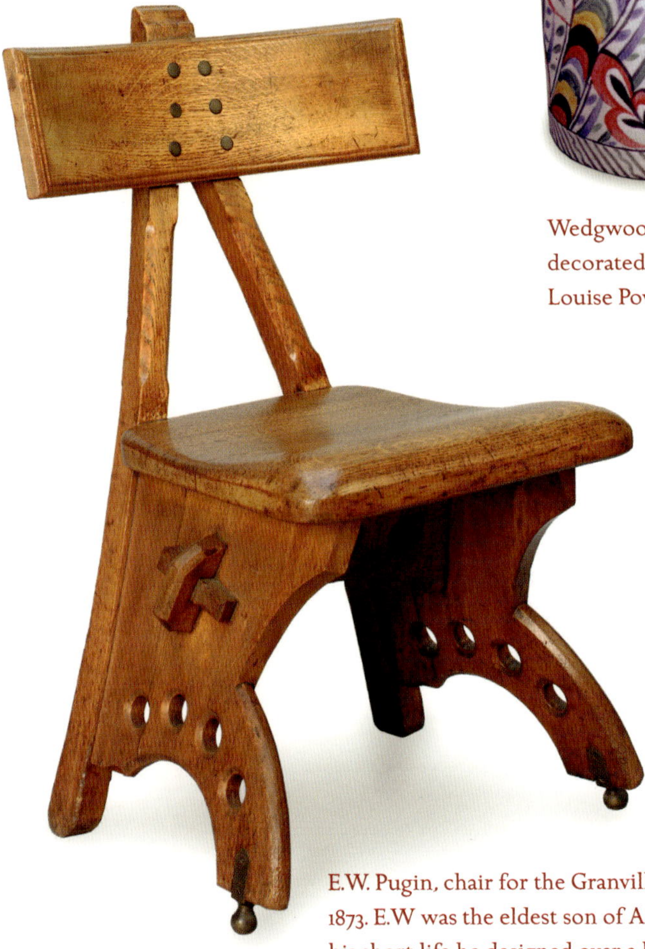

E.W. Pugin, chair for the Granville Hotel, Ramsgate, 1873. E.W was the eldest son of A.W.N. Pugin, during his short life he designed over a hundred churches, many of them in Ireland, but his greatest passion was for the Granville Hotel, Ramsgate, a scheme into which he put money as well as time

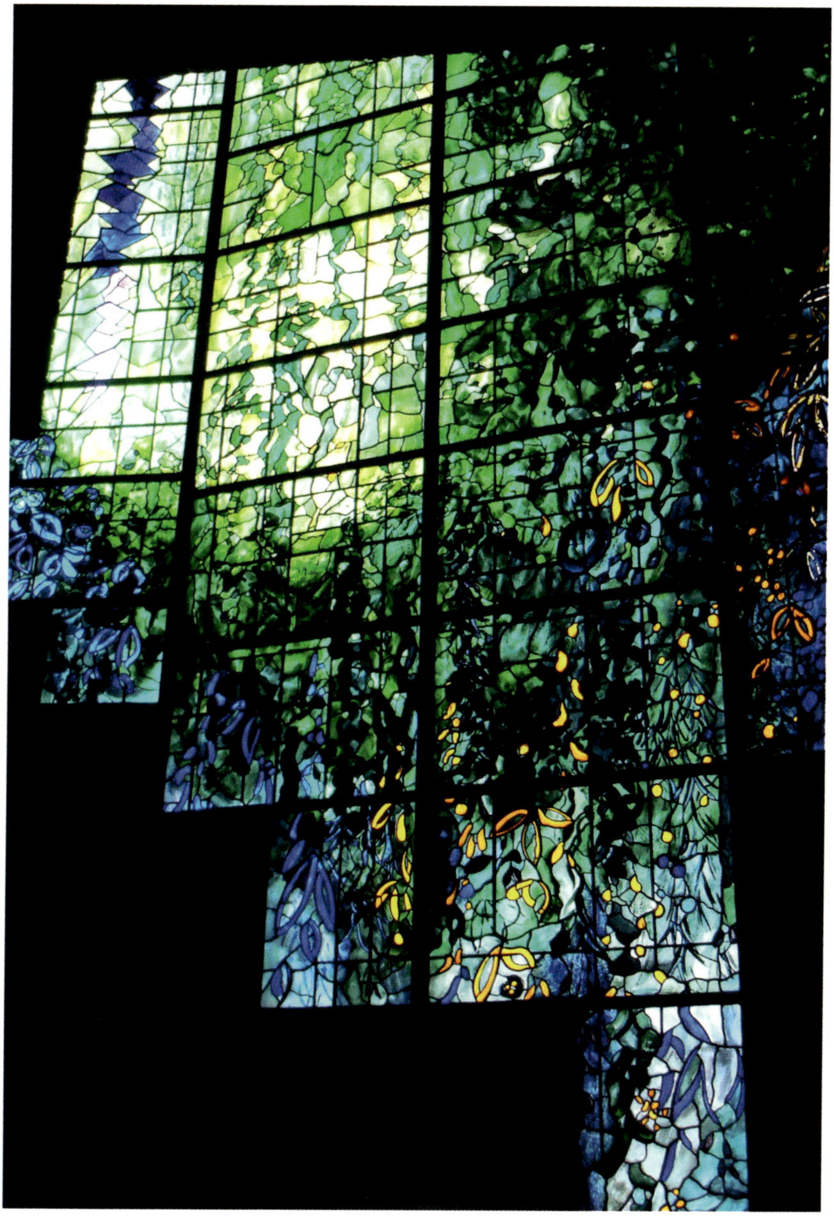

John Piper, *Light of the World* window, Robinson College, Cambridge, 1977-8. For this non-denominational chapel Piper avoided symbolism, creating a peaceful effect of sunshine and foliage

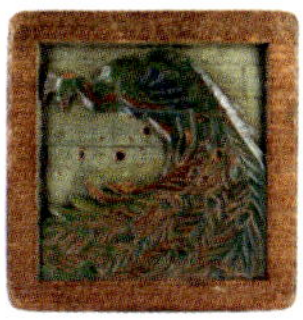

Q *is for...* Quaint, Queens, Quennells, Quill, Quilting & Quirky

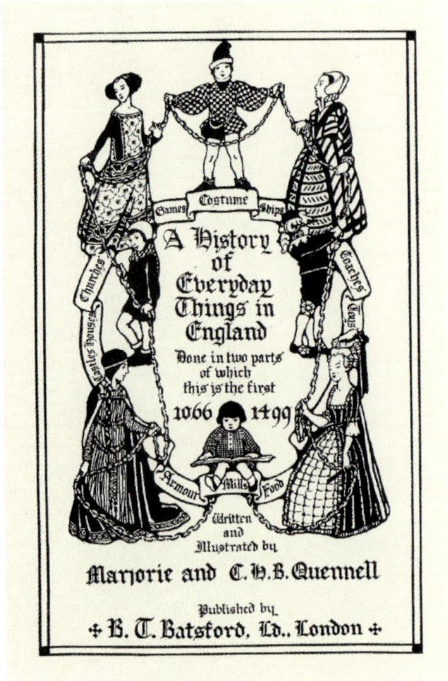

C.H.B & Marjorie Quennell title page to Volume one of *A History of Everyday Things in England* (1918 – 1934) and opposite a C.H.B. Quennell house in the Frognal area of Hampstead, dubbed by Pevsner as 'Quennell-land'

Queen Alexandra Memorial by Sir Alfred Gilbert, St James's, London, 1926–32

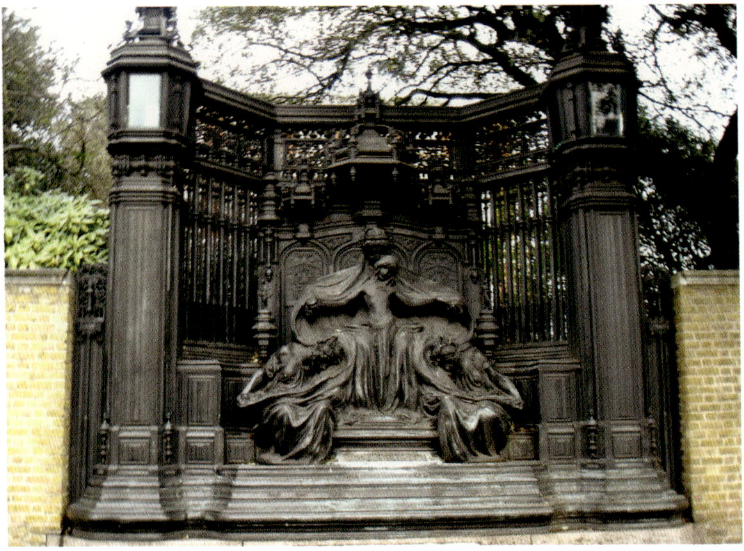

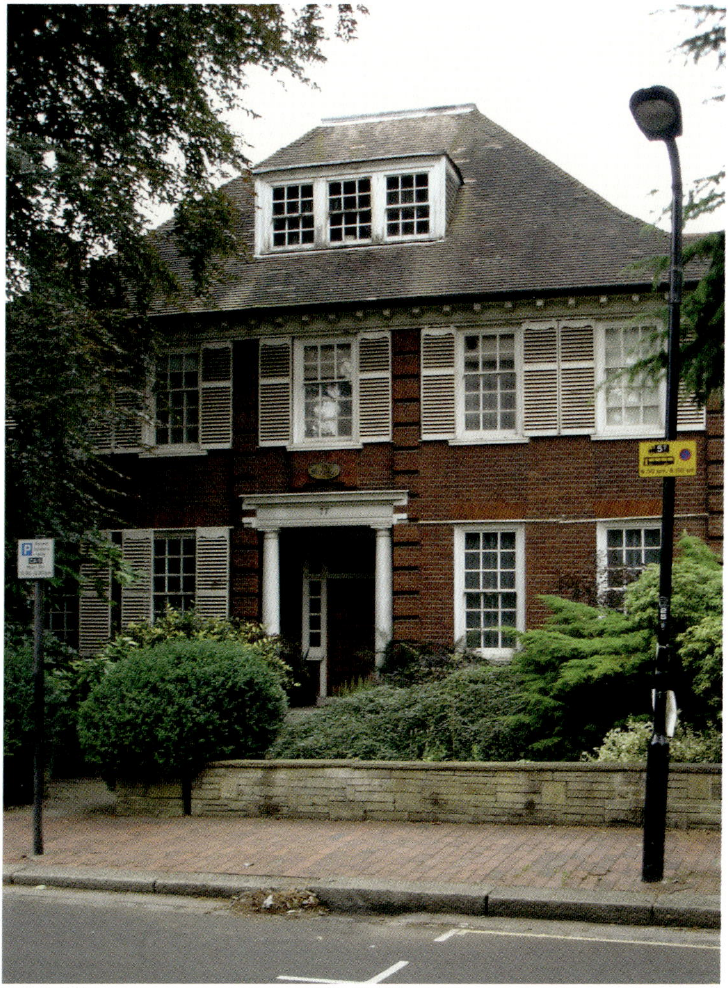

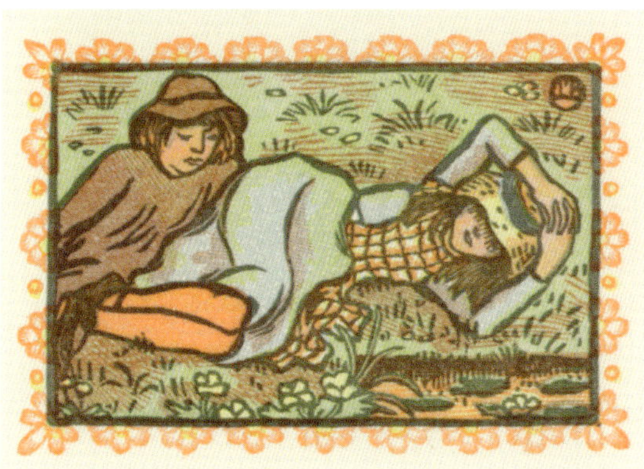

Queen of the Fishes colour wood engraving by Lucien Pissarro for his and Escher's Eragny Press, 1894

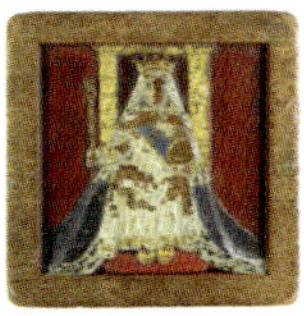

R *is for...* Ramsden, Rathbone, Ravilious, Rawnsley, Reynolds-Stephens, Rhead, Ricardo, Richardson, Richmond, Ricketts, Riemerschmid, Rippl-Rónai, Robinson, Rohlfs, Rooke, Rookwood, Rossetti, Rothenstein, Rowley, Roycroft, Ruskin, Russell & Rutherston.

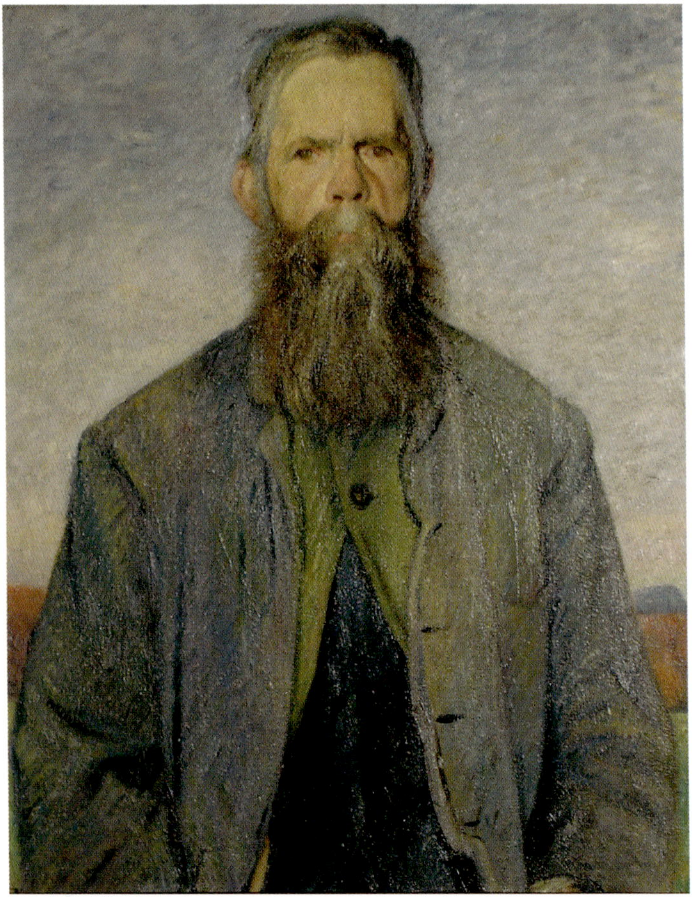

Sir William Rothenstein, *Eli the Thatcher*, 1913. Rothenstein had a house in the Cotswold village of Far Oakridge, and painted and drew many of the local craftsmen

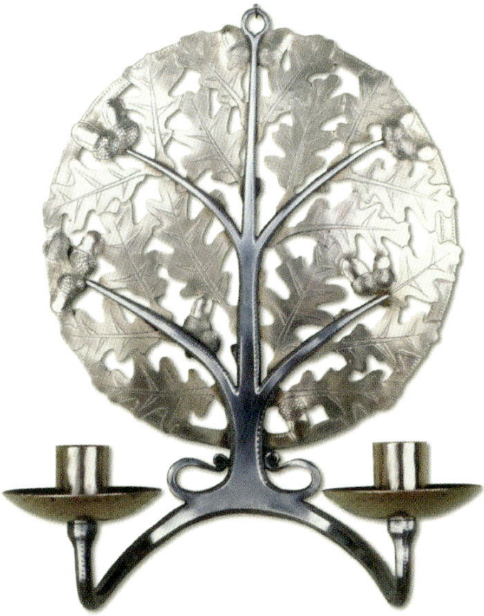

Sir Gordon Russell, iron and brass
oakleaf candle sconce, 1920s

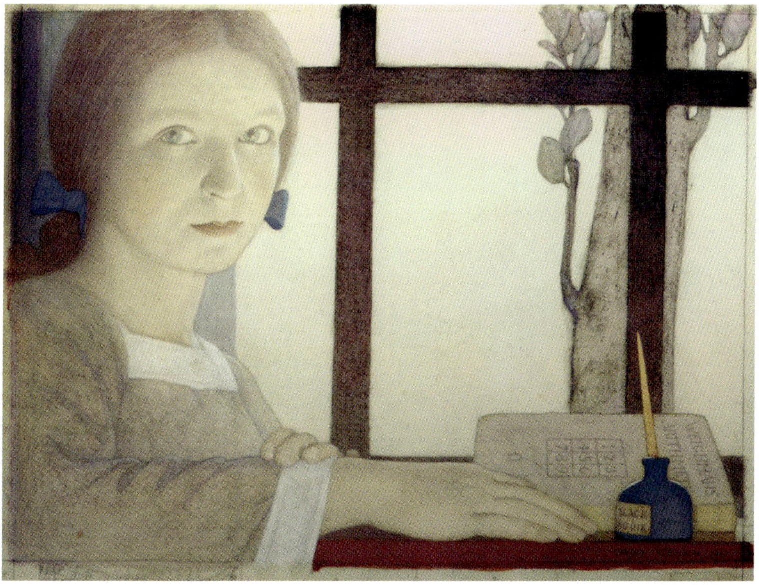

Frederick Cayley Robinson,
Lesson Time, 1921

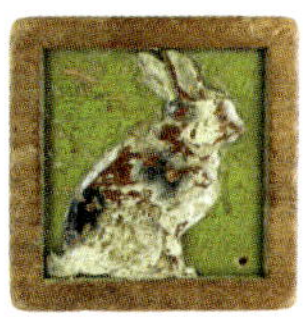

S *is for…* Saarinen, St George's Guild, Sands End Pottery, Schultz-Weir, Scott, Sedding, Seddon, Settle, Shaw, Shannon, Silver, Simonds, Simpson, Smith, Solomon, Southall, S.P.A.B., Spencer, Stabler, Stevens, Stickley, Stirling-Lee, Street, Sullivan, Summerly, Sumner, Sutherland, Swan, Sykes.

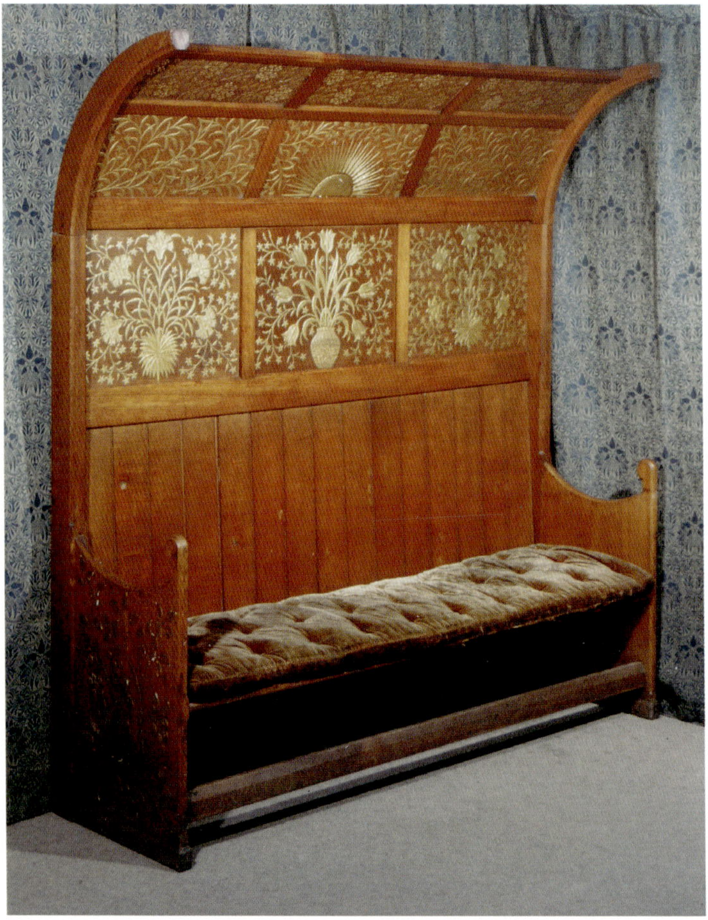

Philip Webb, high-backed settle for Morris & Co. early 1860s. Webb was one of Morris's closest friends and associates. He designed Red House, Bexleyheath for Morris as well as much of the early furniture for Morris, Marshall, Faulkner & Co

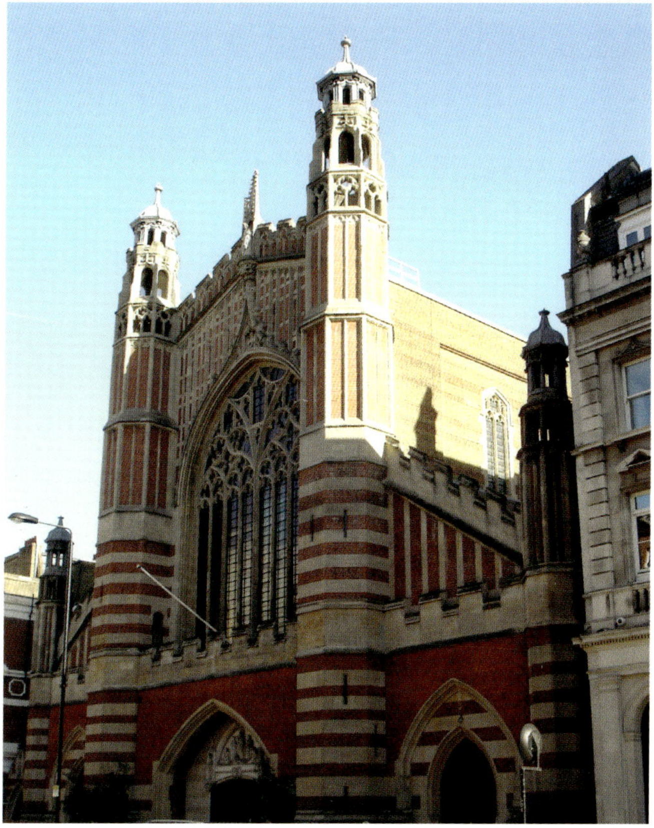

J.D. Sedding's masterpiece, Holy Trinity, Sloane Street, Chelsea, 1889-92, described by John Betjeman as the Cathedral of the Arts and Crafts Movement

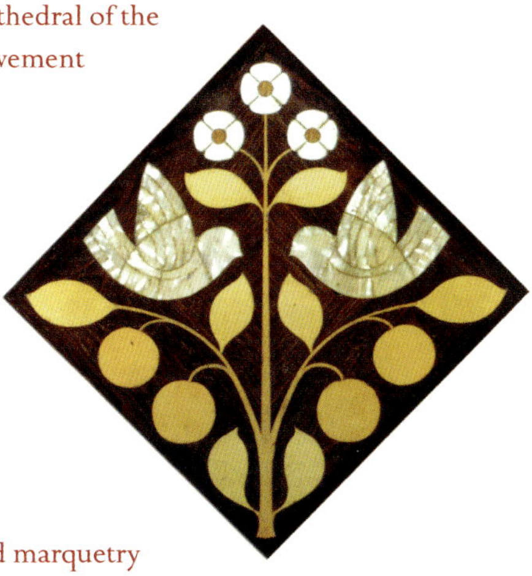

Mother-of-pearl and marquetry inlay by M.H. Baillie Scott

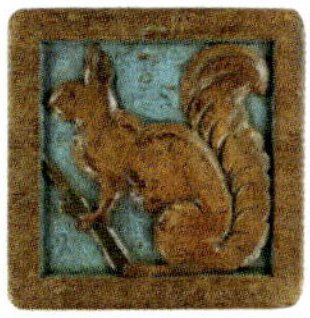

T *is for...* Talbert, Taylor, Tenisheva, Textiles, Thonet, Thornycroft, Tiara, Tiffany, Tinworth, Tolstoy, Tooth, Townsend, Toynbee Hall, Troup, Traquair & Tweed.

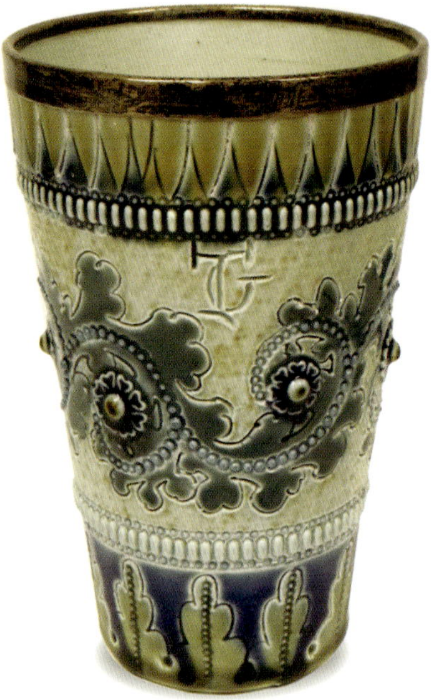

Silver-banded beaker by George Tinworth for Doulton, 1880s. Tinworth's name and reputation are virtually synonymous with that of Doulton's and a street in Lambeth close to the firm's old factory still bears his name

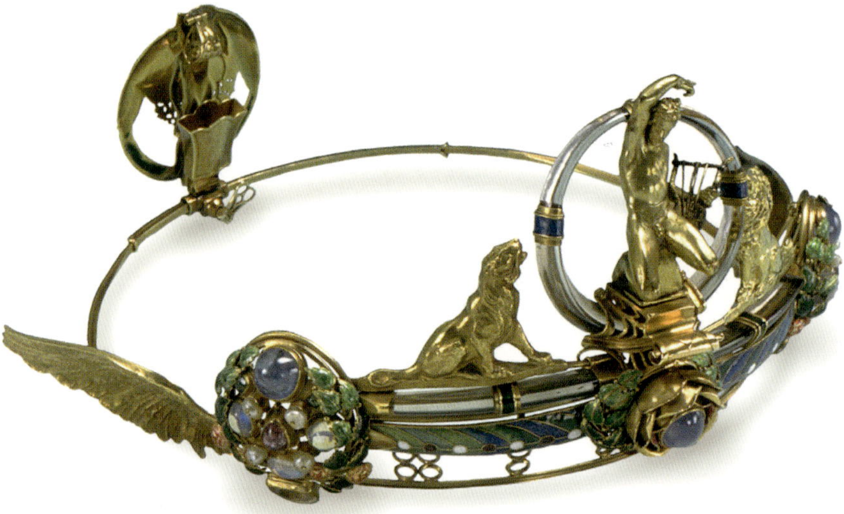

Henry Wilson, Tiara for Lady Llewellyn Smith, 1904

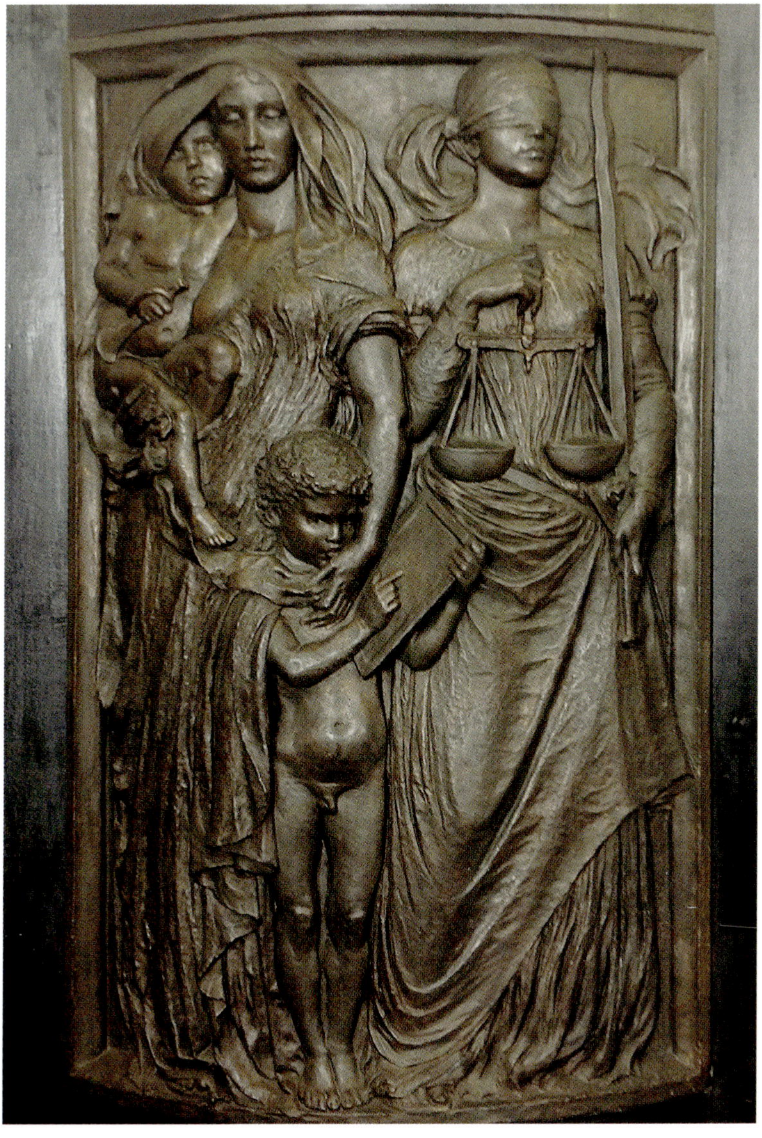

Sir W. Hamo Thornycroft, plaster modello for *Charity and Justice* for plinth of General Gordon Memorial, 1887–9

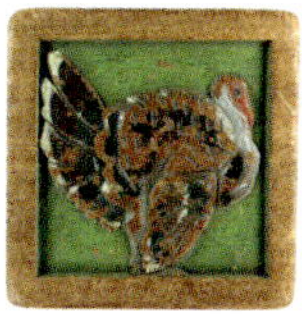

U *is for…*
Uncomfortable, 'Under….', Undi, Unique, Unknown, Unsworth, Unwin & Urishibara.

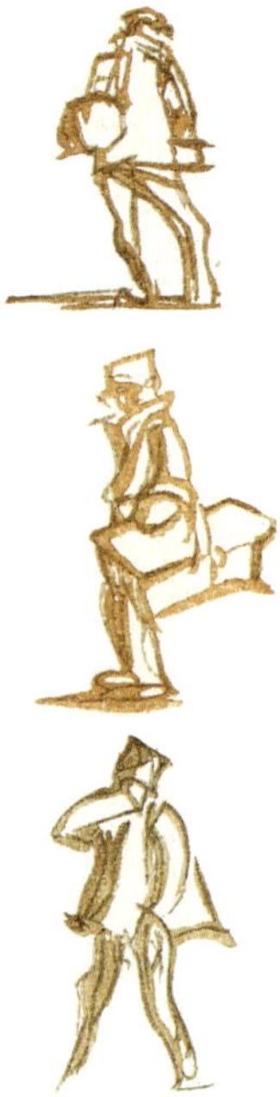

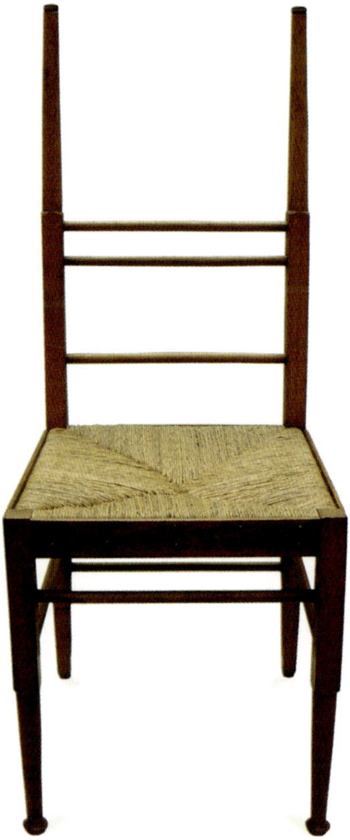

Uncomfortable E.W. Godwin, chair, 1883

Urushibara, woodcuts after Sir Frank Brangwyn, 1940

Raymond Unwin, Hampstead Garden Suburb, 1909–11
Unwin along with his brother-in-law, Sir Barry Parker was the father of town planning in England. His conception for the Hampstead Way entrance to the Suburb was based on the gatehouses of mediaeval German walled cities, providing a clear division between town and country

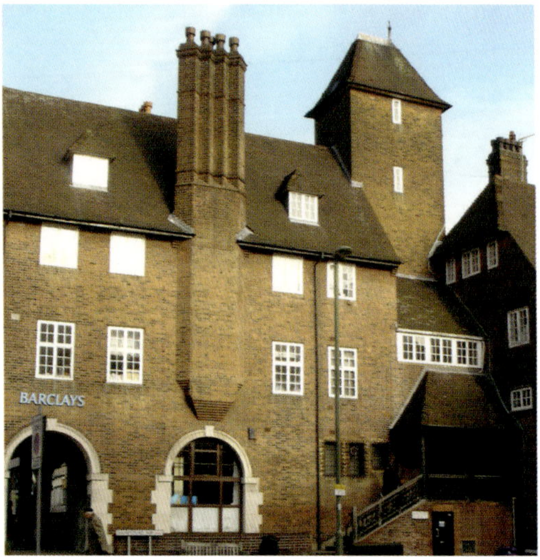

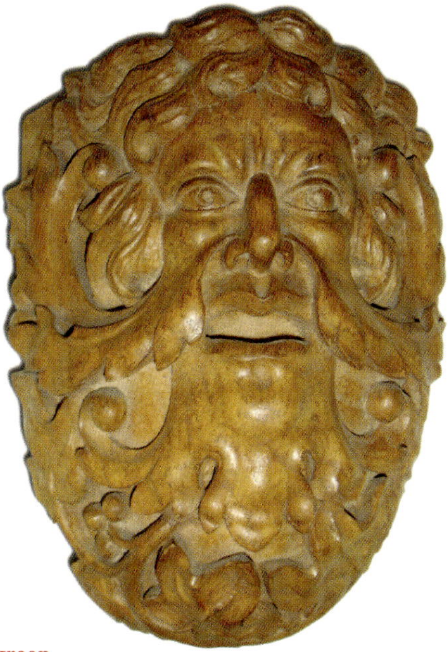

Unknown carver, green man corbel, c.1890

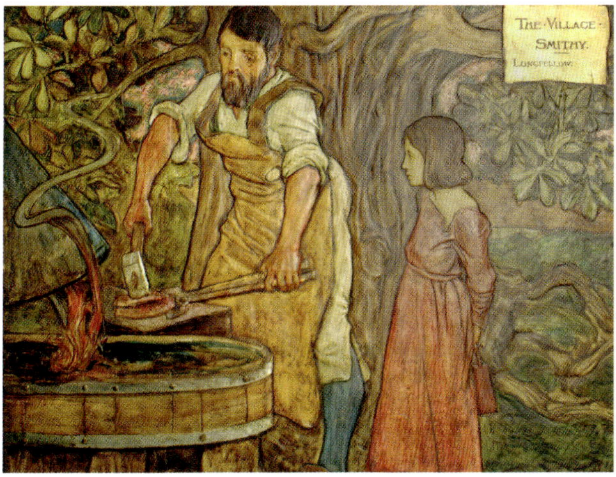

'Under a spreading chestnut-tree / The village smithy stands' (Longfellow, *The Village Smithy*) painted plaster relief by Frank Lynn Jenkins and Gerald Moira, 1898. One of seventeen panels depicting scenes from his favourite authors commissioned by Ernest Hall Watt for the library of his house at Bishop Burton, Yorkshire, designed by G.F. Unsworth

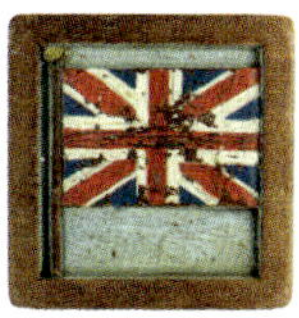

V *is for...* Vallance, Van de Velde, Van Erp, Varley, Vaughan Williams, Vigers, Violet-le-Duc, Voysey, Vrubell & Vulliamy & Vyse

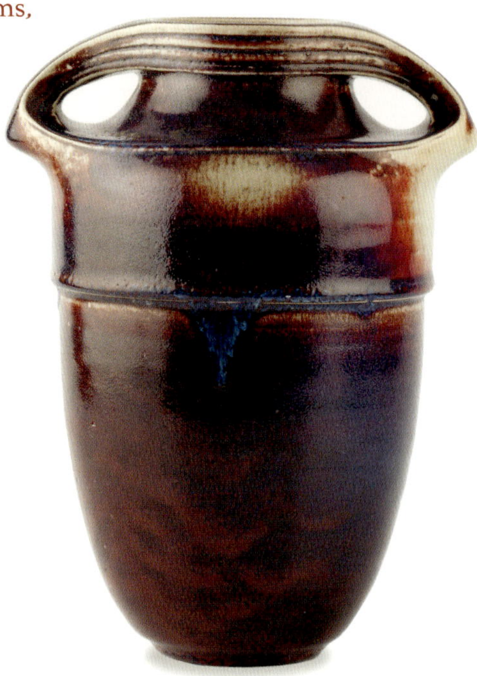

Henri Van de Velde, Sang-de-boeuf stoneware vase, 1902, for the Reinhold Hanke Pottery, Westerwald

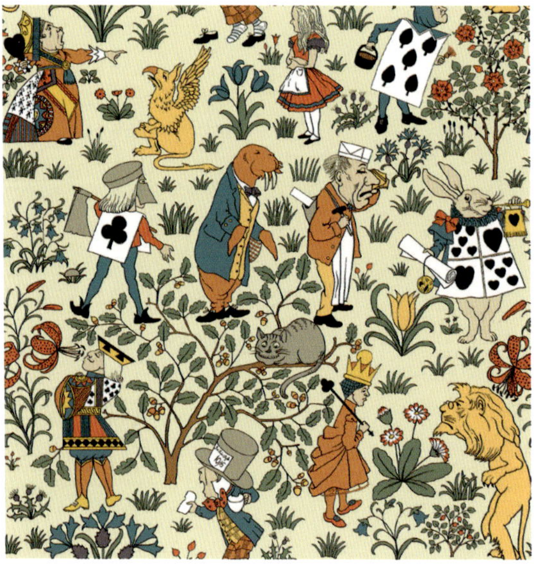

C.F.A. Voysey, Alice in Wonderland wallpaper design, 1930

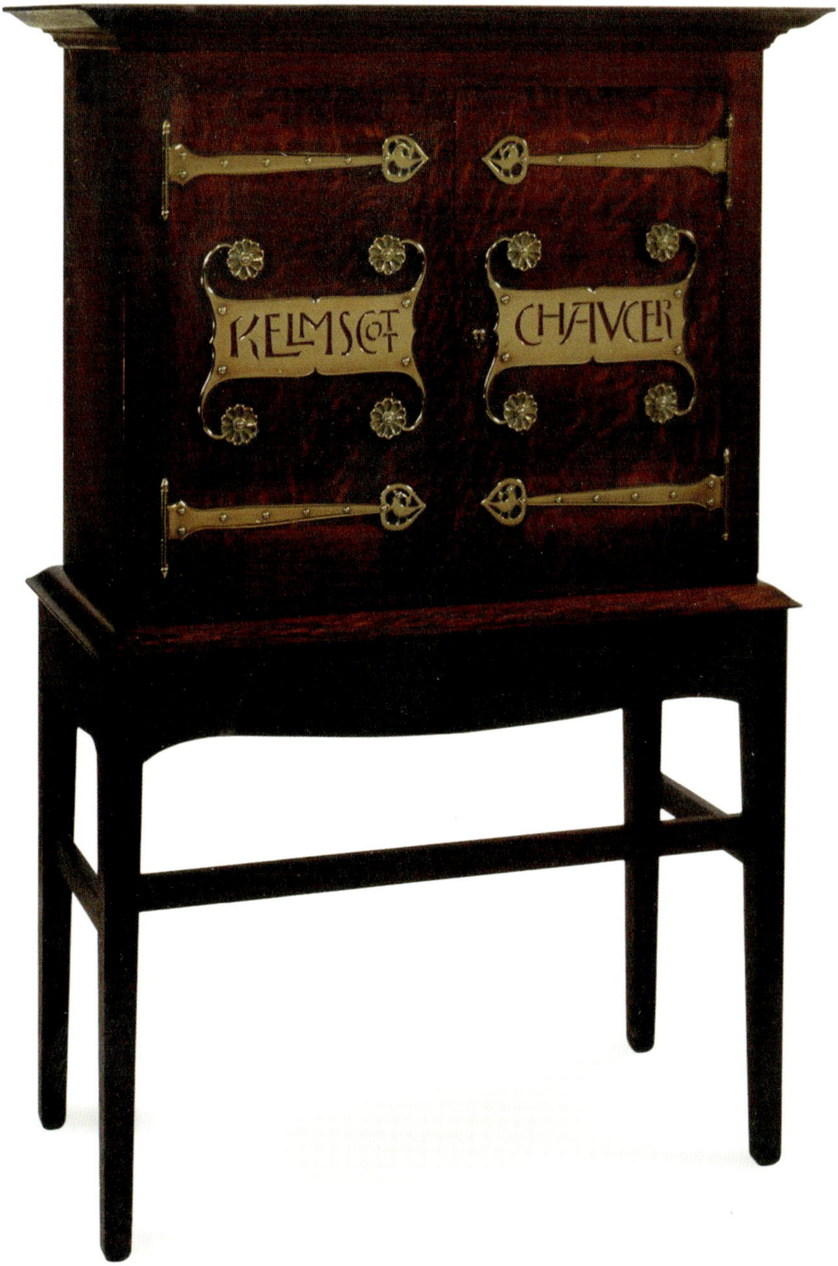

C.F.A. Voysey, 'Kelmscott Chaucer' cabinet, c.1899, commissioned by William and Haydee Ward-Higgs and made by Frederick Coote to contain their copy of William Morris's Kelmscott Chaucer

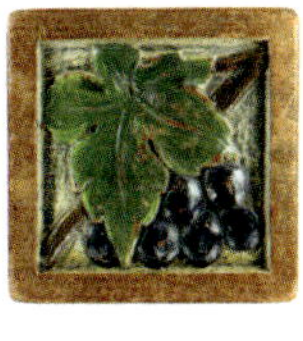

W *is for…* Waals, Walker, Walton, Wardle, Watts, Webb, Wedgwood, Welch, Whall, Whistler, White, Whitefriars, Whitman, Wiener Werkstätte, Wilde, Winchombe, Wilson, Winmill, Wood, Woodroffe, Wright, Wylie & Lockhead, & Wyon.

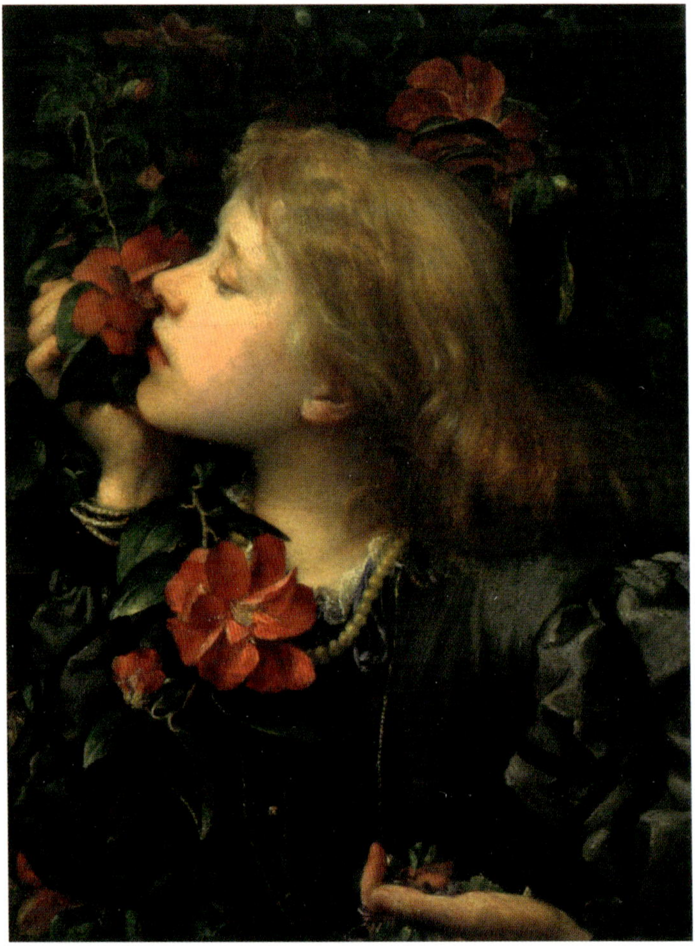

G.F. Watts, *Choosing*, 1864. The eternal enigma: the choice between the scentless, beautiful camellia and the humble, fragrant violet

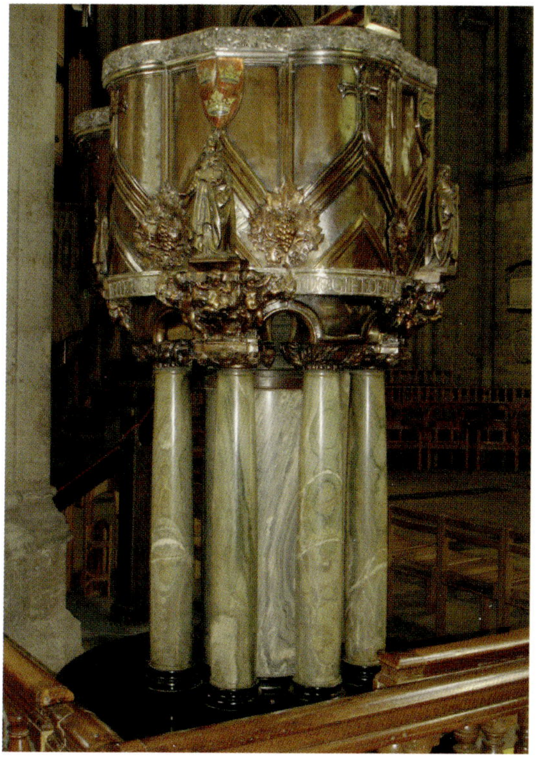

Henry Wilson, bronze, copper and marble pulpit, 1910–13, Cathedral of St Wilfrid, Ripon

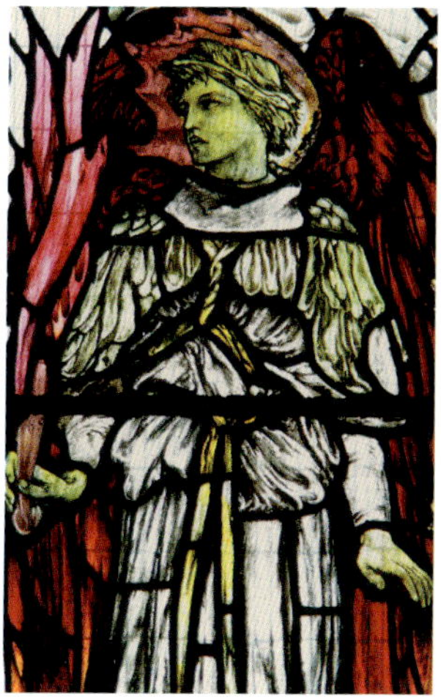

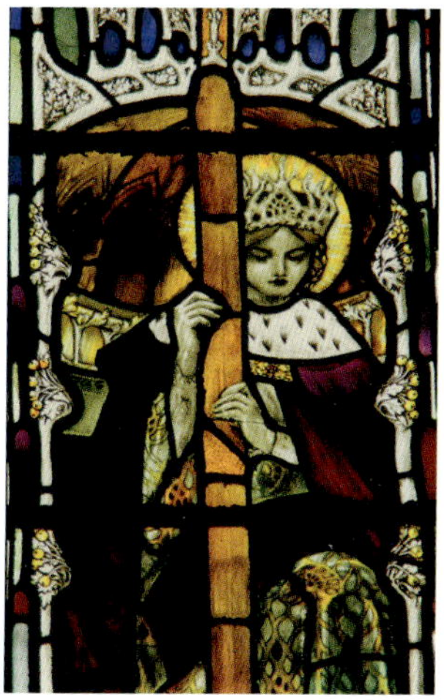

Christopher Whall, stained glass panels, Lady Chapel, Gloucester Cathedral, 1898

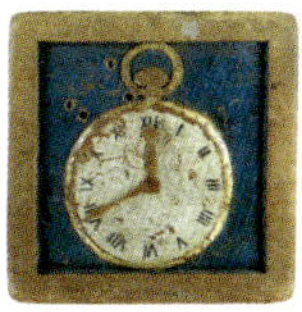

X *is for…* Xerography, X-rated, Les XX & Xylographer.

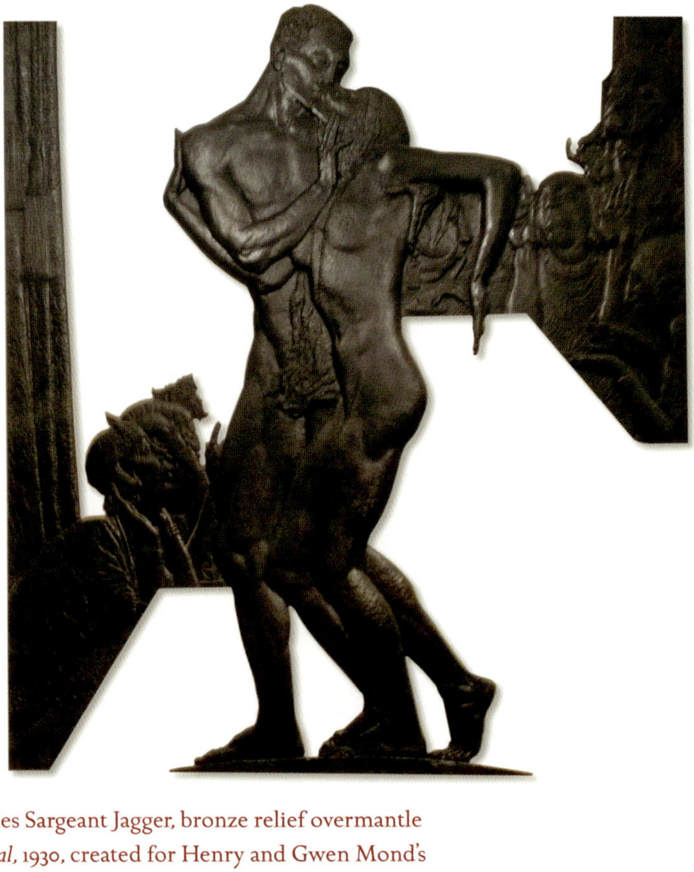

Charles Sargeant Jagger, bronze relief overmantle *Scandal*, 1930, created for Henry and Gwen Mond's house in Smith Sqaure, Westminster. The title refers to the earlier scandalous ménage à trois with Gwen's former lover Gilbert Cannan

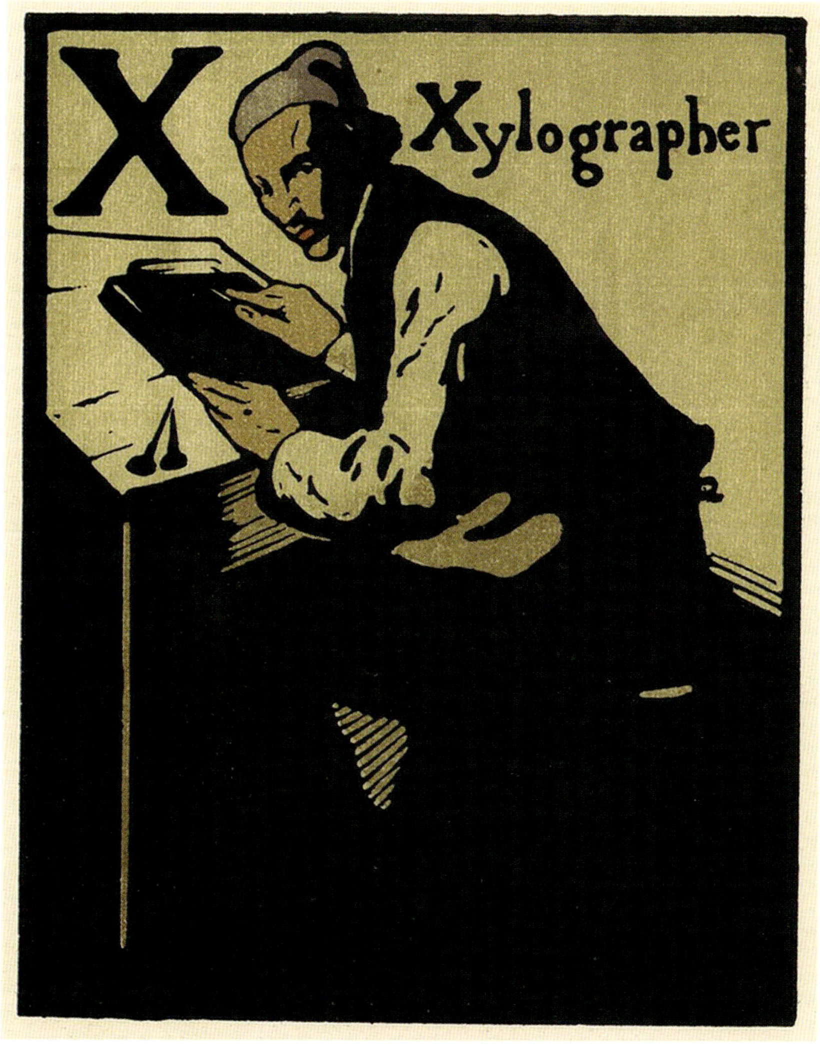

The Xylographer (wood engraver). William Nicholson's illustration from his book *An Alphabet,* 1897. The lithographs from wood-cuts are in the manner of the Beggarstaff brothers, a poster-designing venture founded with his brother-in-law James Pryde.

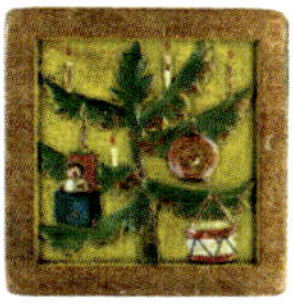

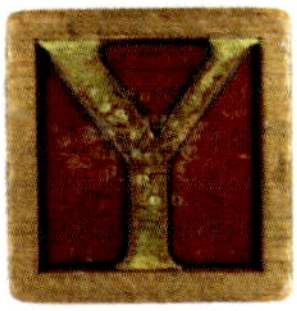

is for... Yacht, Yeats, Yellin & Young.

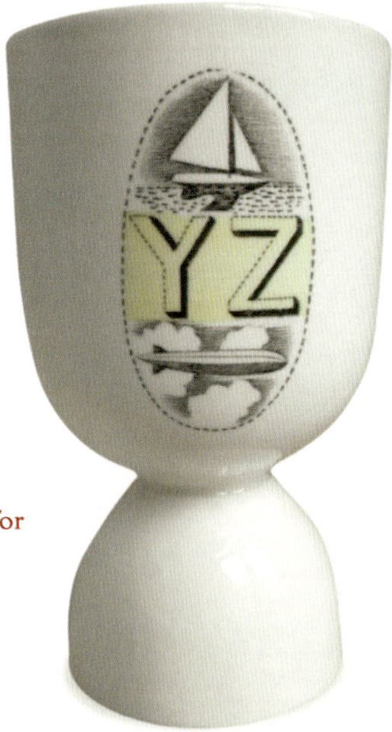

Yacht double egg cup, duck egg size, designed by Eric Ravilious for Wedgwood, c.1937

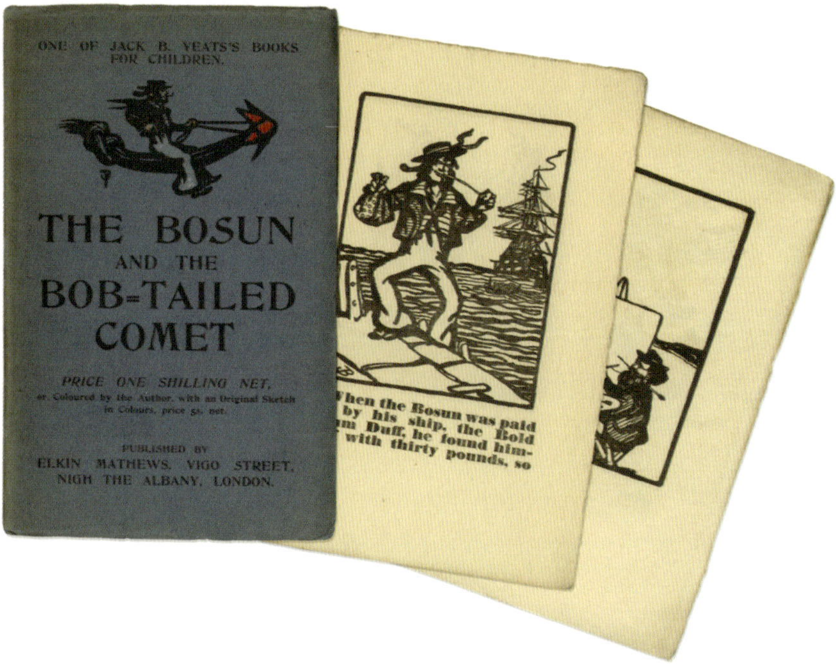

Jack Yeats, *The Bosun and the Bob-tailed Comet*, 1904

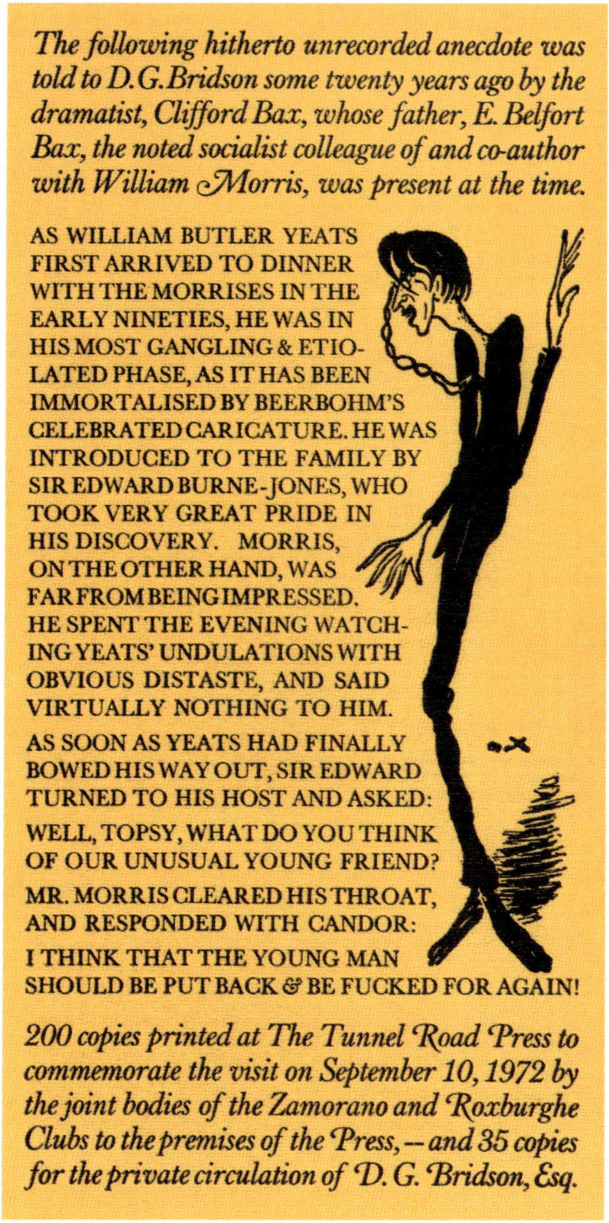

The following hitherto unrecorded anecdote was told to D.G. Bridson some twenty years ago by the dramatist, Clifford Bax, whose father, E. Belfort Bax, the noted socialist colleague of and co-author with William Morris, was present at the time.

AS WILLIAM BUTLER YEATS FIRST ARRIVED TO DINNER WITH THE MORRISES IN THE EARLY NINETIES, HE WAS IN HIS MOST GANGLING & ETIOLATED PHASE, AS IT HAS BEEN IMMORTALISED BY BEERBOHM'S CELEBRATED CARICATURE. HE WAS INTRODUCED TO THE FAMILY BY SIR EDWARD BURNE-JONES, WHO TOOK VERY GREAT PRIDE IN HIS DISCOVERY. MORRIS, ON THE OTHER HAND, WAS FAR FROM BEING IMPRESSED. HE SPENT THE EVENING WATCHING YEATS' UNDULATIONS WITH OBVIOUS DISTASTE, AND SAID VIRTUALLY NOTHING TO HIM.

AS SOON AS YEATS HAD FINALLY BOWED HIS WAY OUT, SIR EDWARD TURNED TO HIS HOST AND ASKED:

WELL, TOPSY, WHAT DO YOU THINK OF OUR UNUSUAL YOUNG FRIEND?

MR. MORRIS CLEARED HIS THROAT, AND RESPONDED WITH CANDOR:

I THINK THAT THE YOUNG MAN SHOULD BE PUT BACK & BE FUCKED FOR AGAIN!

200 copies printed at The Tunnel Road Press to commemorate the visit on September 10, 1972 by the joint bodies of the Zamorano and Roxburghe Clubs to the premises of the Press, — and 35 copies for the private circulation of D. G. Bridson, Esq.

Max Beerbohm caricature of W.B. Yeats, printed by Tunnel Road Press, 1972

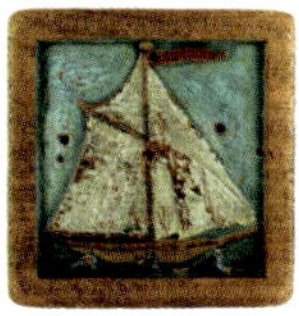

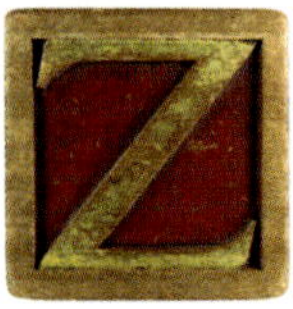

is for... Zeppelin, Zig-Zag, Zinkeisen, Zircon, Zodiac, Zorach & Zsolnay.

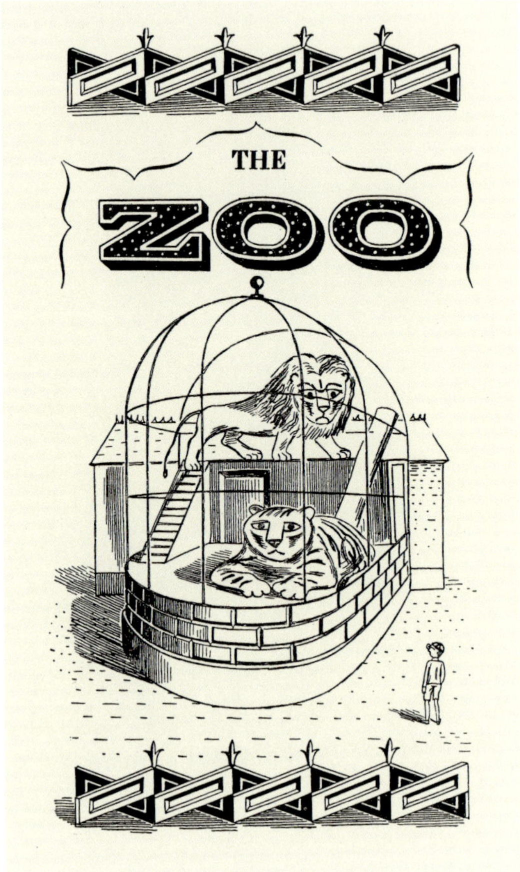

The Zoo, by Edward Bawden is one of the section illustrations to the 1939 edition by Francis and Vera Meynell and published by the Nonsuch Press.

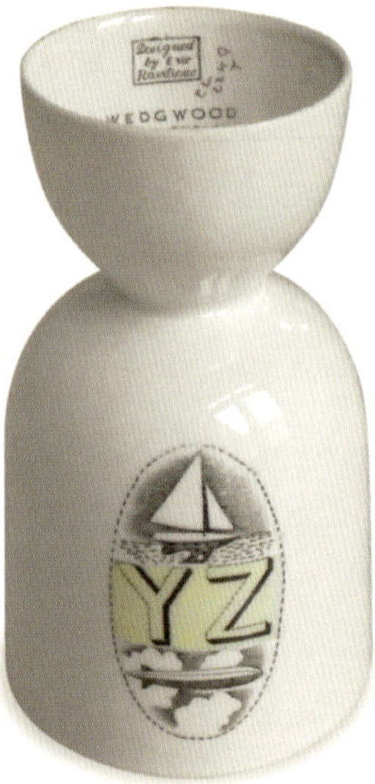

Zeppelin double egg cup, hen's egg size designed by Eric Ravilious for Wedgwood, c.1937. Both Bawden and Ravilious were members of the Junior Art Workers' Guild.

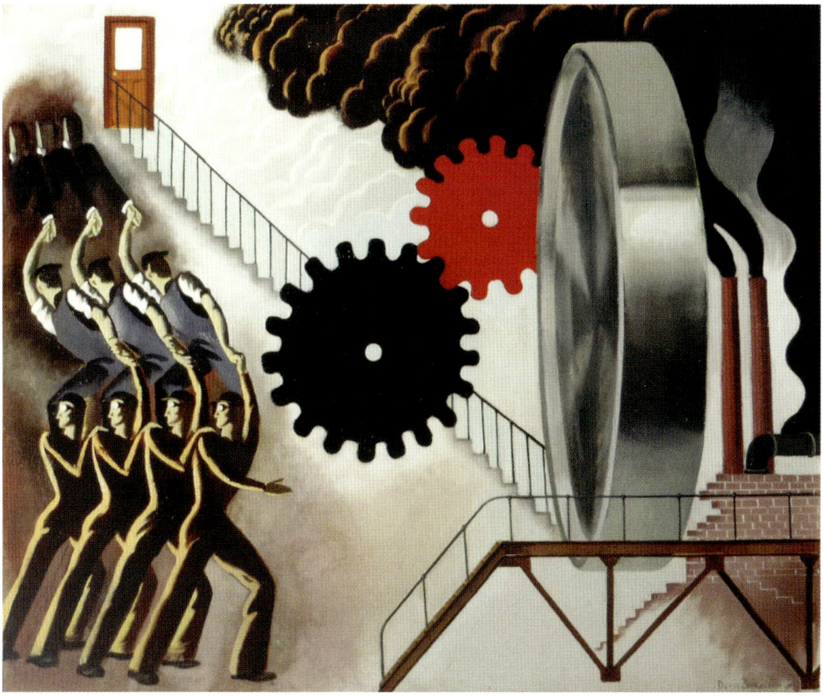

Doris Zinkeisen, mural panel, *The Relations of Management and Labour*, 1944. Doris Zinkeisen and her sister, Anna, produced a wide range of decorative work including jewellery and theatre design, particularly during the inter-war periods

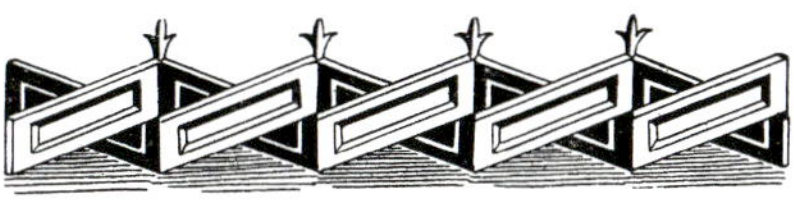

Zig-Zag head and tail piece from Bawden's Zoo

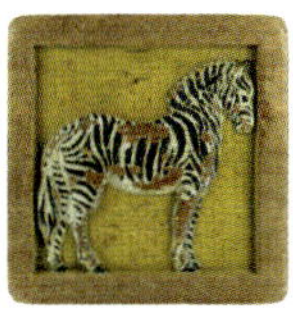

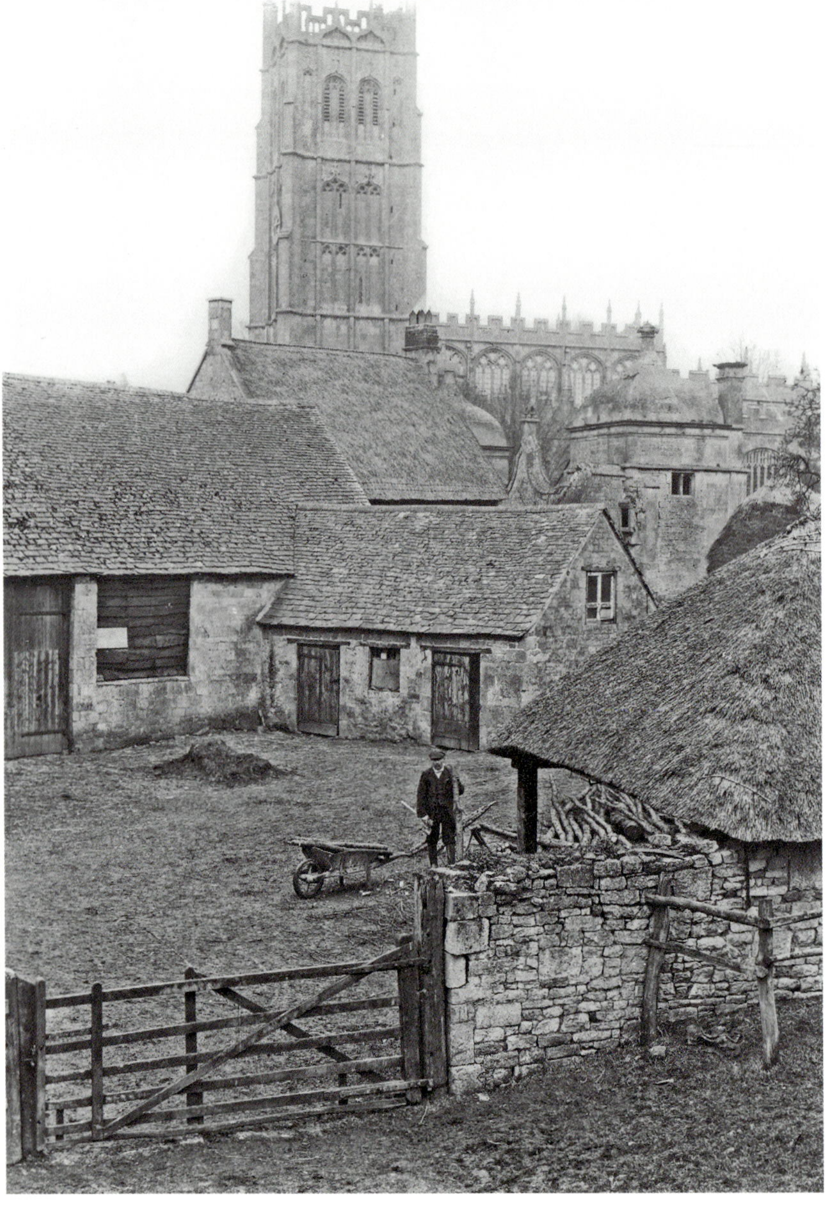

Court Barn with the lodge buildings of Campden House and St James's church in the background, circa 1900 (above) Silver vase made by Derek Elliott of Hart Silversmiths in 2007, to mark the opening of Court Barn (opposite)

COURT BARN IN CHIPPING CAMPDEN

In the beautiful and historic town of Chipping Campden in Gloucestershire a seventeenth-century barn has been transformed into a very special museum, which opened to the public in 2007.

With the help of a generous grant from the Heritage Lottery Fund and a successful fund-raising campaign, a team of local enthusiasts commissioned a conservation architect to adapt the building. The permanent exhibition was installed in displays designed to complement the historic building, and exhibits were lent by several distinguished museums, including the Victoria and Albert.

The former barn now displays a glittering array of silver, jewellery, detailed and delicate woodcarving, etchings, ceramics and finely tooled bookbinding, the work of designers, craftsmen and women who lived and worked in the north Cotswolds from the Arts and Crafts movement in the early 20th century onwards.

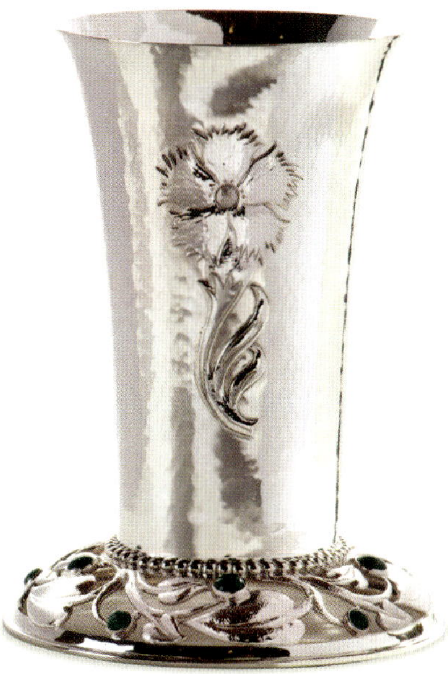

Court Barn celebrates this tradition. As well as work by Ashbee and two former craftsmen from the original Guild of Handicraft, Alec Miller and George Hart, the display focuses on artists, makers and designers including the bookbinder KatharineAdams, the etcher Fred Griggs, the designer-silversmith Robert Welch, and the Winchcombe Pottery.

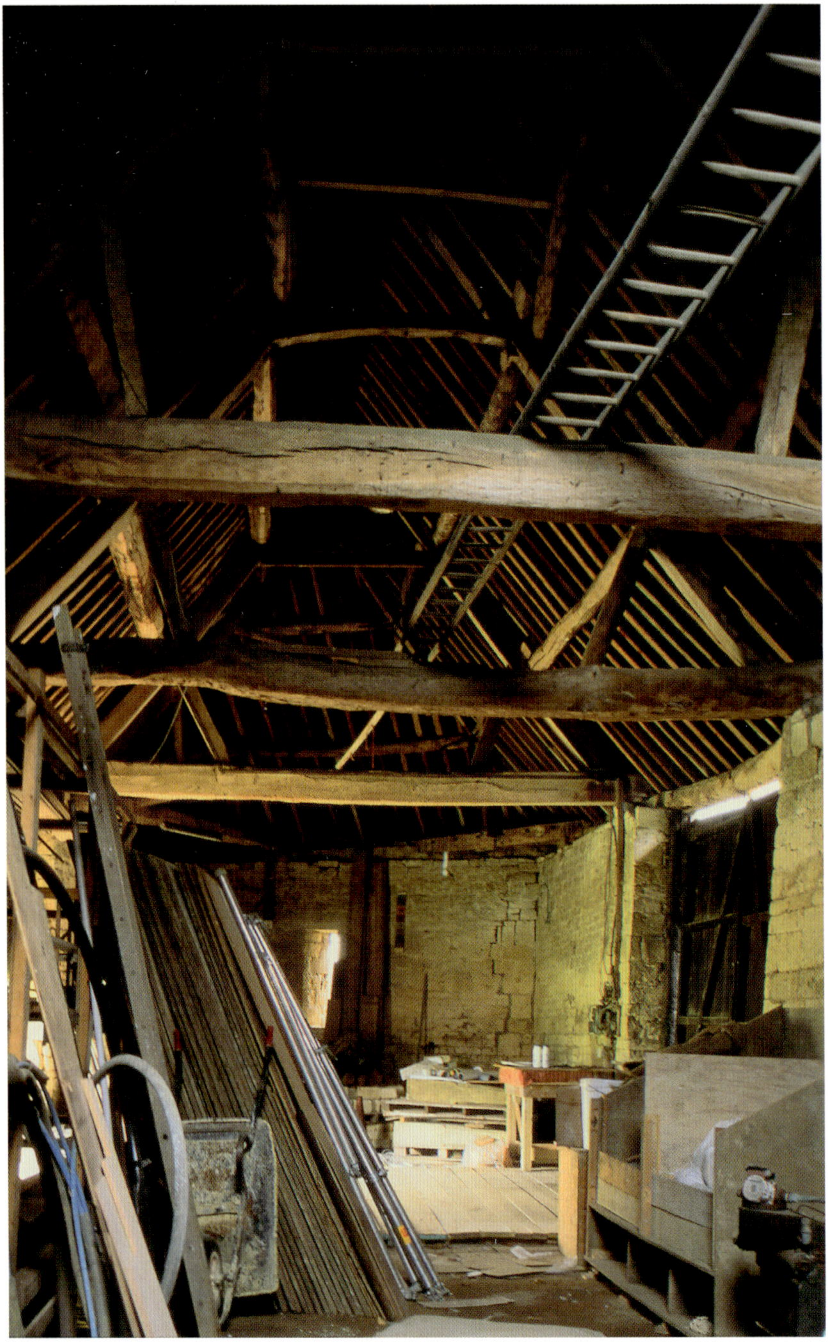

The architects for the restoration of Court Barn were Reg Ellis + Associates, and the builders Pyments of Campden, descendants of one of Ashbee's craftsmen.

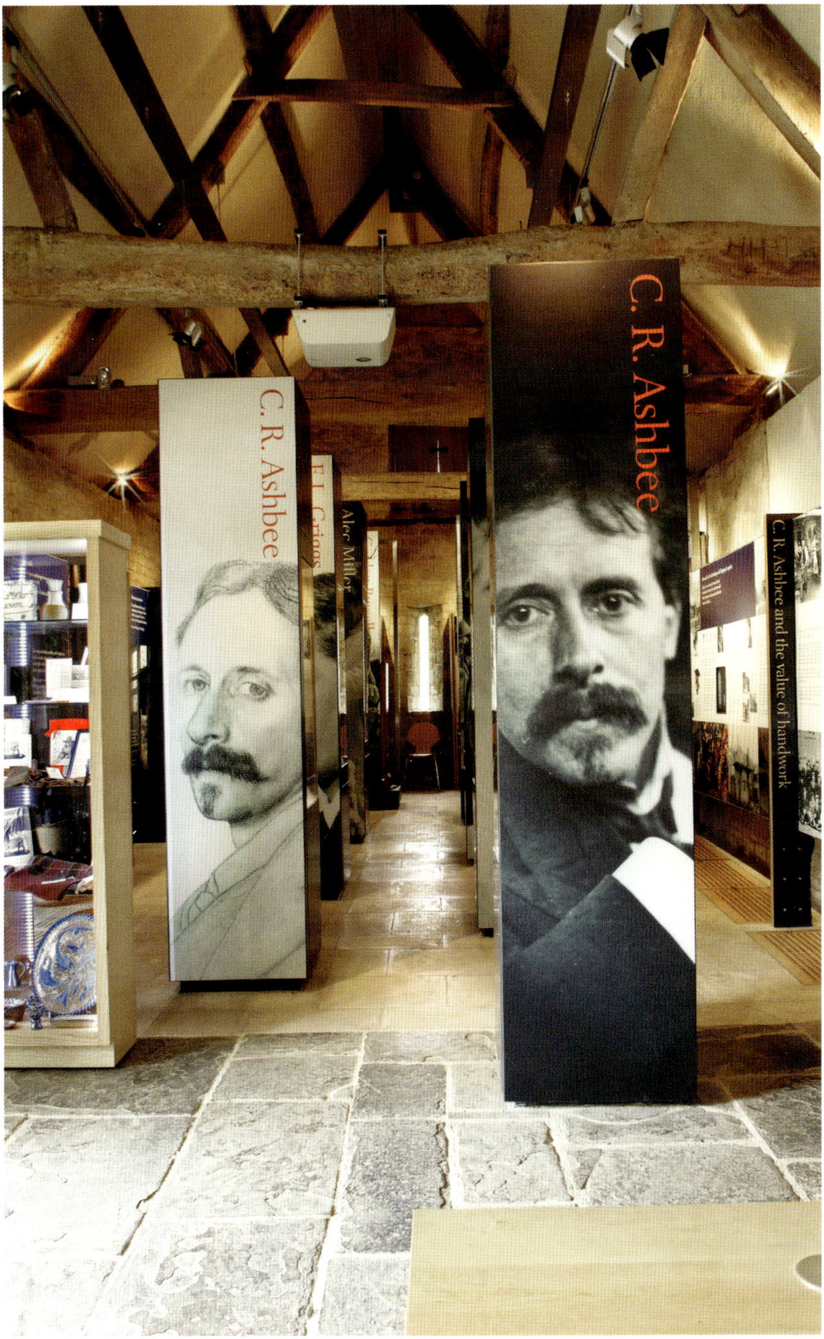

The permanent exhibition at Court Barn was designed by Gareth Hoskins Architects with graphic design by Sue Haigh.

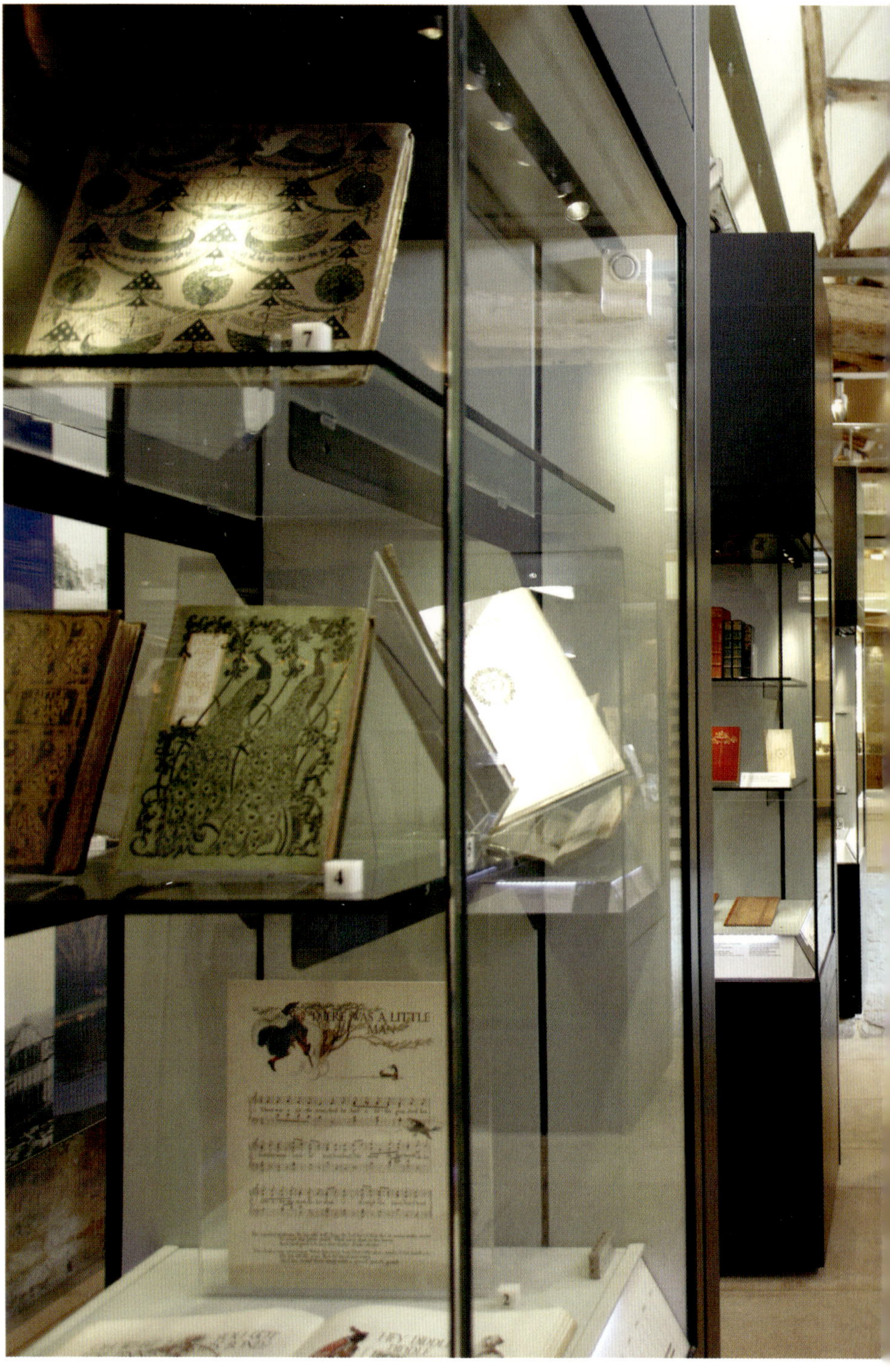
7
4
THERE WAS A LITTLE MAN
2

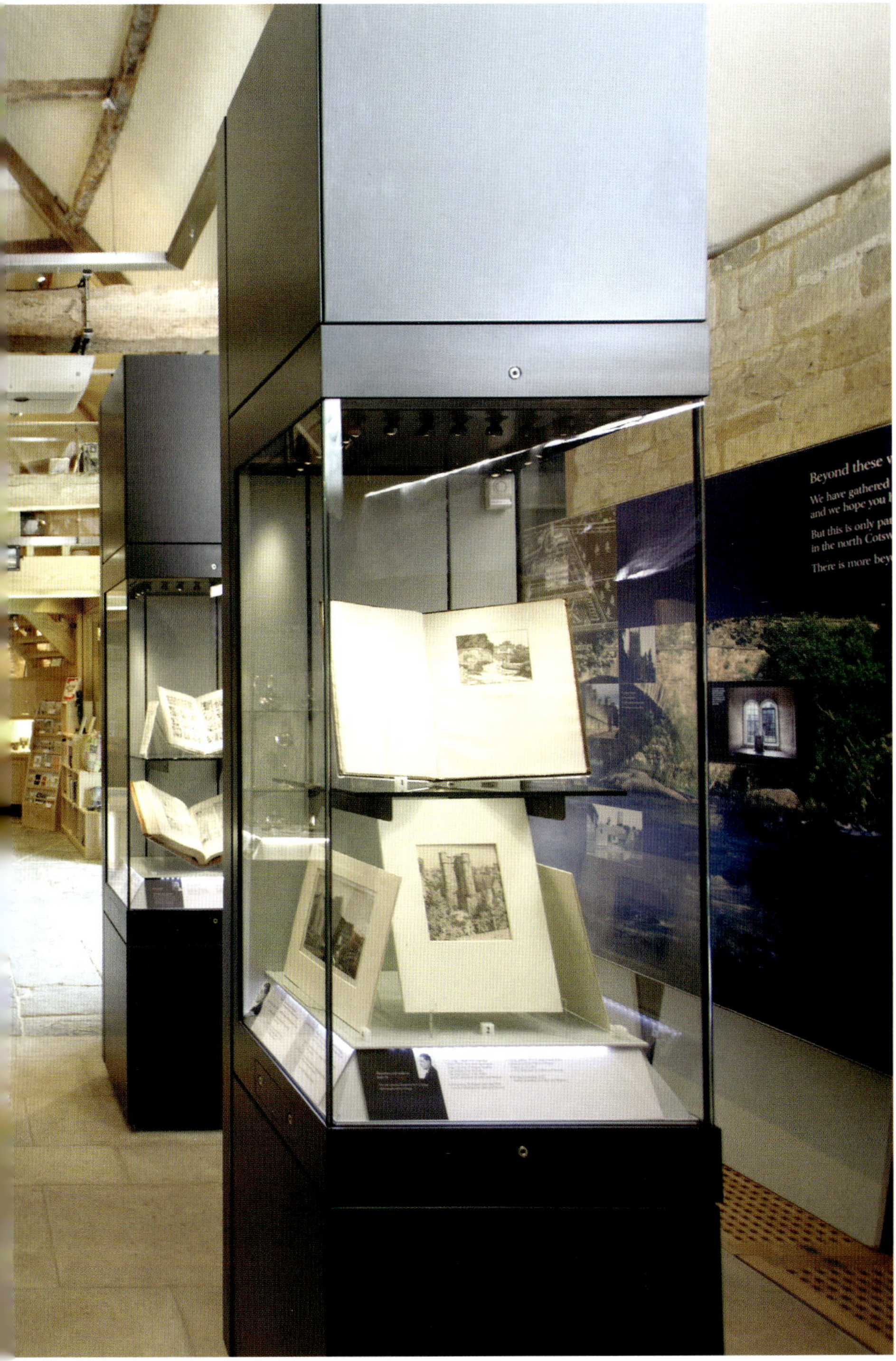

ACKNOWLEDGEMENTS

Photographic copyrights

Art Workers' Guild, 4, 27, 60
Bloomsbury, 48
Cheffins, 9 (top)
Prue Cooper, 9 (bottom)
Peter Cormack, 81 (bottom)
Anthony d'Offay, 65
The Fine Art Society, 36, 37, 38, 39, 40 (bottom), 41 (bottom), 42 (bottom), 43 (bottom), 45, 49 (bottom), 51, 53, 54 (top), 58 (top), 61, 64, 66 (bottom), 71, 72, 73 (bottom), 79, 87
Richard Hookway, 66 (top)
Leicester City Museums, 49 (top),
Liss Llewellyn Fine Art, 2, 18, 43 (top)
Mallams, 78 (top)
William Morris Gallery, London Borough of Waltham Forest, 10-11
National Portrait Gallery, 80
Peyton Skipwith, 12, 14, 29, 30, 41 (top), 46, 47, 52, 54 (bottom), 59, 63, 67, 68 (bottom), 69 (top), 70, 73 (top), 74 (top), 75, 77, 81 (top), 82, 85
Wartski & Co 42 (top), 44 (bottom), 62
Webb & Webb, 13, 16, 50, 56, 58 (bottom), 83, 84, 86, 88
The Wormsley Library, 57
The Worshipful Company of Goldsmiths, 74 (bottom)

Image Credits

Art Workers' Guild, 4, 27, 46 (top), 60
British Museum, 44 (bottom right)
De La Warr Pavilion, Bexhill-on-Sea, 59 (bottom)
Fitzwilliam Museum, Cambridge, 44 (bottom left)
Glasgow University, Hunterian Art Gallery, 61 (top)
Henry Moore Institute, Leeds 75
Leicester City Museums, 49 (top)
Manchester City Art Gallery, 70
National Portrait Gallery, London, 18, 80
Private Collections, 9, 13, 16, 36, 37, 38 (top), 39, 40, 41 (bottom), 42, 43, 45, 48, 50, 51, 53, 54 (top), 56 (top), 58, 59 (top), 61 (bottom), 62 (top) 62 (bottom) (on loan to the British Museum), 66 (top), 69 (bottom), 71, 72, 73 (bottom), 74 (top), 77, 78, 83, 84, 85, 86, 87
Robinson College, Cambridge, 67
Stolen in 1979, Present whereabouts unknown, 64
William Morris Gallery, London Borough of Waltham Forest, 10-11
Victoria & Albert Museum, 38 (bottom), 82
Victoria Art Gallery, Bath, 46 (bottom)
The Wilson, Cheltenham, 49 (bottom), 79
The Wormsley Library, 57
The Worshipful Company of Goldsmiths, 74 (bottom)

The authors would like to thank: Prue Cooper, Peter Cormack, Alan Crawford, Laurence Denmark (Webb & Webb), Mary Greensted, Monica Grose-Hodge and Leigh Milsom Fowler (Art Workers' Guild), Avril and George Hardie, Tim Knox (Fitzwilliam Museum), Sarah McCormick Healy (Court Barn Museum), Geoffrey Munn (Wartski's), Rosemary Ransome-Wallis (The Worshipful Company of Goldsmiths), Pippa Stockdale (The Fine Art Society), and Paul Whitfield, who originated this project.

First Published 2017

Hardback ISBN 978-0-9542824-3-1

Published by The Guild of Handicraft Trust

Designed by Webb and Webb Design Limited, London
Printed in England by The Dorset Press

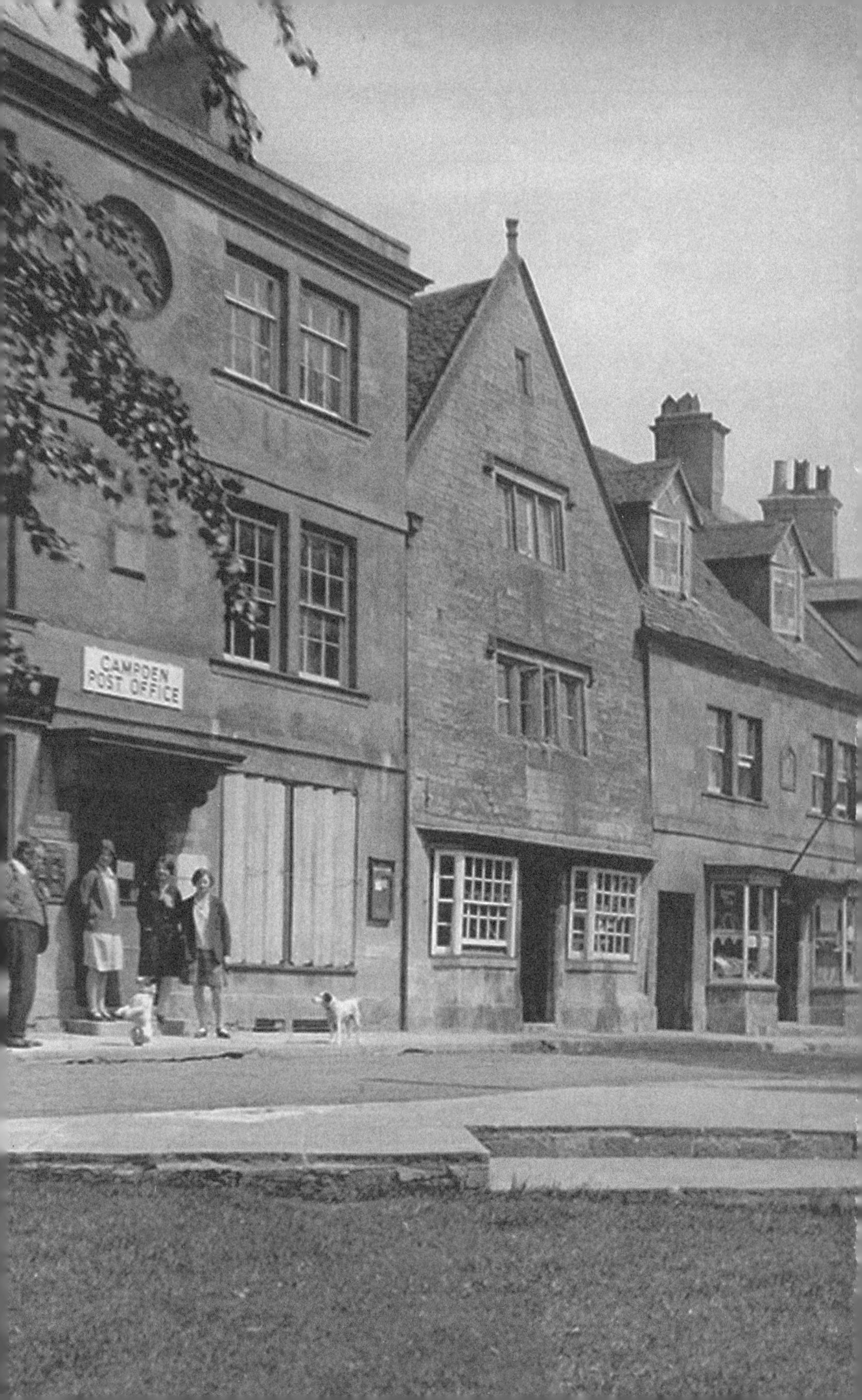
CAMPDEN
POST OFFICE